The typeface of this book is Bodoni 72.
There are 31,330 words in this book.

Published by Meeüz & Purple Heifer Publishing
December 2018 Newport Beach, California USA

Made Genius
Nonfiction.

Made
Genius

A Leigh Corbett

More by A. Leigh Corbett:

Poetry Collections:
The id: The Art of Being Human (2009)
The Life Ever After (2010)
The Writing On the Wall (2010)
Sound Brilliance (2011)
The Life Ever After (2011)
Boundless (2011)
The Drug List (2014)
While We're Young (2015)
The Dark Lamppost (2017)

Fiction (Short):
Forest for A Tree (2015)

Fiction (Novel)
The Lovers Tree (2015)
Boxes (2017)

Non-Fiction:
Wisdom 23 (2014)
24: Wiser Fools (2015)

Table of Contents

This book is dedicated to my both brother and sister

Andrew Corbett
&
Somer Corbett

Thank you for the memories

Made Genius

1
Cold Open

"But I'm not a genius"
I think to myself.

Seems like a silly thought to be having, no? Is it silly because I'm obviously a genius, or because there is no way I could ever really be one?

What is a *genius* anyway—intelligence is a given, but there's something *more* a person "has" that causes people to refer to them as a "genius," and my question is, what is it?

Is it Creativity with a capital "C," or is it something more static, like constant creativity, all lower case letters?
Does creativity even matter?
My guess is that it probably matters pretty significantly.

Geniuses are magical in non-whimsical way, aren't they?
Society seems to think so at least—painting a perpetual archetypal, stereotyped portrait of them: talented, gifted, tortured into greatness and endowed beyond the ordinary "being" with good, great gifts of the gods—a splash of divinity washing over the human soul, whispering in

tender gusts of inspiration and innovation over the lull of their quiet contemplation—"not I" said those privy to its frequency: a "daemon" to the Greek philosophers and "genius" to the Roman ones, rarely did the Ego ever take due or undue credit, at least in regard to such ancient wisdom or artistic creation. To ancient philosophers and artists, these facts of perception were all aspects of universal knowledge—authorless for the self-actualizing.

"How esoteric" I say to myself, concluding my inner monologue and returning to reality.

But I don't *really* return from my mind because I'm not living in your reality and quite frankly, you probably aren't either; I have my own version—and you're welcome to join me.

The thing is about dissecting "Genius" is that geniuses don't really exist. I mean, they do, but also, they do not.

Let me explain:

it's partly the fault of a semiotic paradox, and partly the byproduct of elusive knowledge—We just think geniuses exist simply because we have convinced ourselves that we can "see" them in all the things that they've produced, be it from art, music, technology, mathematics—Lennon, Jobs, Picasso, Dali, Mozart, Eminem (say what you will about Marshall Mathers; (the man is a lyrical mastermind) and yet, we still can't seem to articulate why they *became* different and what factor specifically led to their inevitable success. But we do know that they *are different,* and we can even say "how" in some cases, but why—that's often open to interpretation, isn't it?

They, the geniuses, made a choice to follow their **passion.** Passion is unparalleled in its ability to produce the fantastic in otherwise bleak circumstances or situations, along with perseverance, the outcome can yield unbelievable results. Passion itself is an enduring type of strength that stems from a commitment to pursue all that which fills you with personal pride, peace, and joy.

Once you get a taste of what that is like, very few people would walk away from it willingly—the opposite usually happens, and some people become so consumed by their passion as they can begin to feel the effect unfolding out onto itself.

We all share some experience of initiation into "adult" life from childhood. For me, it has been a long process that at times, educed me to the ashes of manic crashes from some mental high that I couldn't sustain—but that's in a different book.

In this one, we're questioning labels, titles—the unintentional limits we place on ourselves in our daily lives. Let's pretend that genius isn't just a title that we use as a placeholder to describe characteristics of creativity that we don't yet understand. Instead, let's say that genius is a definitive trait—something you have a predisposition for.

When I first began writing this, I was much younger—not just in the literal sense, but both cognitively and emotionally (No shit?). It would seem they are mutually exclusive, but I could also provide a handful of instances where that would not be the case.

Those whom have worked with me personally, especially if it was within the last few years, would likely tell you that I am an "eccentric" genius—which came as a surprise to me but not others; after all, this is my "twelfth book" being published as my fifteenth at the ripe age of twenty-seven, literally about to be twenty-eight.

Hopefully, it was twenty-seven. (it's going to be twenty-eight).

I turn twenty-eight on next week's Wednesday and it is the Monday of this week; I'm on page three of "editing," which is quickly and obviously becoming a rewrite. (It is now Thursday of this week and I came back, again, to the third page.)

This happens a lot—the "rewriting" thing.

It starts off simple, benign: "oh, I'll just read a few pages, maybe some *minor editing.*"

Four hours later and I'm lost in my own oblivion; a minor eternity unfolding as I keep rewording this same sentence a hundred different ways—none of them the correct way, of course. Then I realize the paragraphs are out of order and I really don't like the way the sentences are flowing—hours devoured with ease. Perfection is unattainable, and yet, many of us strive for it daily. I certainly do but have yet to achieve it.

here's what I can tell you:

My MFT (psychotherapist) throughout high school, Richard, met with me during the latter-half of my undergraduate college career, where I was still studying creative writing at Chapman University in Orange—coincidentally located just a few miles down the road from his practice.

I had imagined how our meeting again would go—things were different than they used to be years earlier; my emotional wounds stopped bleeding and started to finally heal. I still had a long way to go in my healing at the time, but I'd already made so much progress from where I started. That much was obvious.

Richard couldn't stop smiling the whole conversation, "you're so different than you used to be" he finally says after about an hour. And even though I knew he was right, and why, I still asked him "what do you mean?" anyway. I needed to hear it, to be affirmed in my actualization process.

"Well" he says reflectively, "you seem happier, calmer. You're almost like another person now" and I'm certain that he's right; that is exactly how it felt. I've become another person *even now* from *then*–I've felt myself endlessly transforming through the different lessons, trials, and tribulations of my life.

Sometimes, those difficulties facilitate the opportunity for a better sense of self...and sometimes for a worse sense of it; I try to stay away from those dark places; I don't need that negativity in my life, actually. And no, I do not regret anything, but there are some portions of my past that serve no other purpose for me other than to memorialize the outcome for why I should never be that way.

Speaking of transforming and truth, one of the most simple truths of life, that I have found empirically, is that I cannot ever really lose what I truly *am*, therefore my "nature" will always follow *within* me wherever I go *outwardly*–and beneath the pain exuding itself through emotions un-tame was this optimistic idealist convinced it *still gets better*, some how, somewhere–but I have to *get there* first.

Getting there.

That's the real story here, isn't it?
It is.

Intelligence and emotions are not mutually exclusive. I do not believe that geniuses are simply born and can grow haphazardly into achievement—the amazing beauty of the brain is its ability to compensate and react to its needs being met or unmet in an environment.

Geniuses, as they appear to others to be, are made in a moment—and then they have beautiful, transcendental instances that at times, is sustained for a lengthy duration. But the brilliant brain does not live its life in isolation inside a clean room, it's bound to an emotional life that its body is living with it—experience everything all the time everywhere, whether its consciousness is aware of it or not; geniuses are born in a moment, and only when the conditions demand it manifest itself through the "will" of a capable outlet—artist, musician, mathematician, writer, or otherwise. Genius can of course happen repeatedly, and that kind of ability, as creativity in a specific subject area, can of course be conditioned. But there seems to be a limiting factor that undermines the entire intention of labeling someone or something a "genius."

Part of this book is "how" I became who I am today and why, and whether you agree with my concept of genius. But if I were to whole-heartedly commit to the assumption that my siblings and I are geniuses, then the question is, can you see the outcome developing in our childhood?

Some day, I hope that someone might be reading these words and relate or be so curious, that their open mind opened their latent potential to achieve extraordinary things.

Maybe you'll hate this book.

However, this next part *is* important—if it is the last thing you do in this life, you **must** absolutely find your passion.

And if you're not sure if you know the experience or if you have never felt what passion engulfing your soul is like, then keep looking; it's out there.

SUCCESS IS LIKE RAINDROPS

Do I feel accomplished as a writer?

Not really, not yet at least. I do not have a best-seller nor a cult following; both of which are suitable outcomes for a great success. So in terms of achievement, I feel like I've been perhaps a tad lazy to be quite honest, especially as of late. I haven't even transferred my poetry from paper to a word document—something I used to do habitually as part of my process—so I could be actually only half-writing all these "finished" poems...

However, I remind myself that I also produce a lot and to stop and glance back at the path I'm leaving behind:

Success is like raindrops—you feel little parts of it at a time in different places, but if you look around, you can sometimes see the effect what that's doing—which is getting water everywhere, if it's rain.

If Malcom Gladwell (author of *Outliers)* had ever met me, he'd likely call me an outlier after examining my story and throw me in his pile of misfit geniuses, but the term "out*sider*" feels more familiar.

I was a whopping twenty-five years old when I began writing this, and at the time, I believed I had all the "non-answers" to all of my questions, but time has proven a more virtuous adversary. The duration from "first writing" to that last stage of editing has revealed a dramatic shift in my style and approach to life.

Which brings me back to the original question, and the branches of questions erupting from it:

What is genius?

Is there a difference between genius and prodigy during childhood—and what's the defining factor there? Is it prolificacy or creativity, or both?

When we say "genius," do people really mean extraordinarily creative and gifted?"

If so, why then does MENSA think that three-digit number next to IQ is so important, if that same brain might never achieve its full potential?

Is labeling someone a genius condemning them to high expectation that they may never feel capable of achieving, or does it empower them to fulfill it?

Are the über-talented youth that continually perform beyond the highest "standard deviation" destined to be the same ones who make the leap from prodigy into perceived genius come adulthood, or can a genius simply...manifest itself spontaneously? And if so, is there a specific age this must occur by—or is genius purely a "younger person" phenomena?

My Parents: Jim and Trudy

2
BIG Questions

There's this question circulating between the academic and scientific communities regarding the idea that "genius" is something that the environment *made* rather than something the individual was *born* with; several longitudinal studies have been conducted and the conclusion yielded results stating that a higher IQ merely makes one *intelligent*, **not** a genius—genius has something more, and the question of what "*more-ness*" a genius has that others do not has now become the focal point of most discussions—genius is only apparent as an *after-the-fact* phenomena because the judgment of "genius" is based primarily upon what is *produced* by the individual, and the *effect* that their production has on its respective community thereafter its initial impact—meaning that we don't actually yet know how to identify genius while in its infantile form—which begs the question, can exist if we don't know how it can be measured?

By "exist" I mean in physical form as a specific, distinct genotypic trait that is either expressed or suppressed, and if it is expressed, would always "on" if activated. From my perspective, anyone can be anything, and people can be geniuses without being a "genius," in the sense that they are experts and notably more successful than most others, but they may not breach that abstract threshold into where Einstein and Steve Jobs are standing.

For example, Einstein was considered an idiot by his math teacher before he was ever considered a genius by anyone else. Einstein's high school math teacher assumed that he must have cheated on the math exam, when in fact, his student was actually *smarter* than him. The teacher couldn't comprehend the thought-processes that young Albert had provided for his answer, and the adult's intuitive response to confronting raw talent and brilliance was to fail the student – misunderstanding geniuses during their earlier years was not uncommon because their thinking is often judged or confused with crazy or "out-there" people.

> "Everyone is a genius, but if you judge a fish by its ability to climb a tree, it will live its whole life believing that it is stupid." – Albert Einstein

Maybe there's something to what Einstein is famously quoted as saying—but can we prove it?

Both Andrew and I had our intelligence questioned, tested, and analyzed in the form of formalized, in-person IQ tests—more than once, and at different stages of our development. Somer in contrast, displayed no developmental delays or challenges, and therefore, had no such testing conducted. Somer regularly scored in the 99th percentile for most of her academic standardized testing. It is important to take note that only a certified neuropsychiatrist is qualified to administer such testing in regard to intelligence; the IQ internet tests, no matter how intensive they may seem, hold no validity in comparison.

Ultimately, IQ tests serve really only one valid purpose in the realms of neurology and psychiatry, and it is for identifying cognitive deficit. In terms of test capacity and plasticity–there is much room for improvement, and there is no way to anticipate or predict achievement in terms of "works produced" in a given subject–from an IQ test.

Creativity is subjective and unpredictable; yet, it is objectively measured, isn't it?

The issue with this type of objectivity is that it yields a subjective assessment that can never truly be "objective" since it is inherently referential.

I have been formally tested by a neuropsychiatrist–trust me when I say that you are *exactly* what you make yourself to be; all it takes is the **decision** and the affirmative choice to **follow through**. Raw "will power" can accomplish difficult feats, if only you believe in the outcome you desire.

Sure, I have written in the range of somewhere over a thousand poems, many of which are published, but that just makes me prolific–not necessarily a genius, or does it?

Sounds impressive?

It doesn't always feel that way necessarily. Anything I'm not "working on" is something that I should've worked longer on.

This book is a case and point for such an example:

Does talent matter to success, is it age-based—are some people born to be destined for greatness, or can it be manufactured—could it be created from the most fundamental characteristics of personality?

I remember hearing my educators discuss my learning predicament—illiterate at the conclusion of third grade, "there's no way she is going to make it through high school" one says to another, "She's a lost cause..."

Funny, isn't it?

THE RESEARCH

In spring of 2016, 92Y hosted a conference called *The 7 Days of Genius* which featured panels of people discussing genius in its various forms.

Carl Zimmer, a columnist for *The New York Times* newspaper asked a panel of experts "do you think neuroscience is giving us some answers as to why some people have it and some people don't?" Heather Berlin, a neuroscientist, answered him saying that "there's a huge genetic component involved." In terms of genius, "you're looking at a combination of somebody who is born with a particular predisposition to have a talent, plus the practice.

So for you, you could practice from now until tomorrow and you'll only get to be so good as a concert pianist. But if you were doing that plus you had this predisposition, you might get to really far extremes and people might call you *genius*." But she also clarifies that, "it's not necessary to have some sort of psychopathology in order to be a genius, and people conflate these two ideas."[1]

Neuroscientist Joy Hirsch also said at the *7 Days of Genius* conference that she "[loves] the idea of the vision that there's a way to, to bring out the genius in all of us...and I wish there was a way in our educational system to develop ways to promote our creativity."[2] Joy goes on to say that "I think the study between individual differences is a really interesting direction to take—difference in say, there's some people who have extraordinary memory...we learn something about what makes one person better at memorizing things than another. There are differences in...how well we can put things together and understanding the rules for those differences is important."

---

[1] *New York Times* columnist Carl Zimmer interviewed Heather Berlin at the *7 Days of Genius* conference which was produced by *92Y* in partnership with *Big Think.* http://92yondemand.org/the-neuroscience-of-genius-creativity-and-improvisation-with-heather-berlin
[2] *New York Times* columnist Carl Zimmer interviewed Joy Hirsch at the *7 Days of Genius* conference which was produced by *92Y* in partnership with *Big Think.* http://92yondemand.org/are-geniuses-born-or-made-with-dr-joy-hirsch

A Professional's Interpretation

Richard, MFT, told me during our sessions that my brother and I were incredibly similar; later, he disclosed that we could even be a case study for addiction and genius because the only other person who experienced the exact same childhood as me is now dead.

Andrew died at the age of 21.

I was 18 years old at the time and fifteen minutes away from the location of his overdose—but I didn't know it was happening. I told him to call me; it was also just two weeks following my high school graduation—which Andrew incidentally missed, and ironically so, because my Dad told him not to come high.

"Why'd you tell him not to come?" I asked my father.

"He's high—he can't come here high" he says with practicality.

"It's *my graduation*—I wanted him here."

"I can't enable him—" my dad pleads as I interrupt him.

"—And I only graduate high school once—and now he missed it."

"There will be other graduations" he says reassuringly.

But there wouldn't be, not for Andrew to attend at least.

I still wish to this day that he would've been there, and my dad unintentionally took that from me, whether or not he was aware of that consequence at the time is uncertain.

Regardless, Andrew still called on my graduation day right after the ceremony ended to tell me that he really wanted to be there at that moment, and he was even going to come before he got in an argument with our dad that day--- which my father just told me about. Andrew said that he "didn't want to spoil the day by upsetting 'the parents' with his presence." I understood.

"I love you Andrew, thank you for remembering and calling. I'm happy you called—means a lot to me" I said to him.

"I'm so proud of you Alexa. You're going to do great things..."

Then I take a moment to reflect: Have I fulfilled his prophecy yet?

To understand the beginning of all of us, or me, you need to understand how Andrew's story came to it's ultimate conclusion first, and why that forced me to transform a—it isn't sunshine and rainbows:

From Richard's analysis, in a "cliffnotes" version, the main difference between Andrew and I was passion and grit.

I had this "insatiable passion" ready to engulf anything that fascinated me—first it was the weather (I'm serious, I had a barometric gauge etc.), then came art, but man, horses were the most magical creatures I'd ever seen! I fell in love the instance I saw one up close and made contact. And what about writing? Well, I've always written, since as long as I can remember, and well before I could read, which usually entailed improvised explanations of things I'd already "wrote."

In contrast, Andrew loved video games and reading. He even attempted long-form writing a few different times, and he started a fictional story once, but eventually lacked the necessary discipline of following-through with it, and it is a long process—don't let me fool you.

> [Ironically, my father attempted to write a book in the 90's about how to be successful in business, but he also never finished it due to his elaborately busy schedule. Then he lost the manuscript and any writer can empathize with that feeling of loss over work incomplete. I found my father's unpublished manuscript in 2018 inside some old boxes at my mother's warehouse, and I returned it to him to finish—I hope.]

If Andrew wasn't finishing Stephen King's latest novel, he was completing the last level of the most newly released game, which was usually some version of Dune, Half-life, Age of Empires etc. We'd play multiplayer against each other sometimes, which is where I would basically become a training-pawn waiting to be destroyed in every possible way for his "practice." I was hardly a worthy opponent. In Age of Empires, I would get nuked out of existence during my dark ages—meanwhile Andrew is 5000 years ahead of me and has space travel. He would even contribute to my resources and I *still* lost—He was that good and I was also *that* terrible. He tried coaching my strategy, and our games got longer and longer but I never won. Not once.

The common theme associating Andrew's activities was an alternate reality—or an escape from his current one.

Reading could take Andrew to other worlds, and the video games were an outlet to move freely in a world with finite rules that could be "cheated" and manipulated to his benefit—unlike the "real world" where the consequences are much more significant and impacting.

As Andrew got older he wanted more friends his age, not just a little sister best friend, and he had a difficult time fitting in with his peers—Asperger's syndrome but high functioning. He failed to cope effectively with the changes.

It started with alcohol.

I was first to notice.

I told my mom but she didn't believe me. I was too afraid of how my father would react to tell him about it. I didn't want to get Andrew in trouble—I wanted to help him.

He frequently kept a bottle of Jack below his bathroom sink; "it's for mouth wash" he tells my mother—she, of course, believes him. I took it upon myself to repeatedly hide the alcohol in places he couldn't find. I knew he'd be too mad at me and flip out if I had actually poured the containers out, so I settled for this not so subtle passive aggressive behavior to show my disapproval. That way he knew that I knew.

DISCOVERY ACADEMY: THE DEATH TRAP

Andrew didn't start using "harder drugs" until he came back from Discovery Academy in Provo, Utah.

Discovery Academy is a terrible, dangerous place. Imagine "wilderness" camp with no wilderness and devout "Mormons" as your "trees."

Never go there.

Tell everyone you know to stay away.

Andrew hated that hellhole and told me they tortured him there. The cryptic letters I got (they read the mail, like prison) made me cry. Real, normal Mormons are not that bad.

These crazy Discovery people put kids (they were all under 18 and over 12) in this small dark closet for hours at a time and called it "detention," for example.

It wasn't uncommon for kids to die at the school in mysterious ways either; there is a large number of unexplained deaths linked to Discovery Academy and the dark web has discussion boards about it. Andrew's death is on there, with the others.

Andrew finished high school as quickly as his genius brain would allow—which was a two years earlier than his trajectory would've been back home at Sage Hill in Newport

Beach, CA. He vowed never to return to Utah again, and he never did.

In retrospect, that was the completely wrong place for him to go. Andrew needed professional help, but not from that wretched excuse for a correctional facility; I'm convinced it gave him PTSD.

Andrew was autistic not a psychopath; he needed stimulation not sensory deprivation. But it doesn't really matter though now, does it?

That's mainly what contributed to Andrew's death, in my opinion—that, and feeling forever inadequate in the eyes of his father. My father had high standards, but those expectations weren't necessarily things Andrew was incapable of; it's just my father wasn't very vocal about praise back then when him when *did* do something adequately.

After a year of meandering and trying his hand as a loan officer and spending all his money on drugs, Andrew went to rehab, twice; the first time he got kicked out pretty quickly.

The second time he did "30 days," allegedly, because when I re-read his old notebooks, they tell a drastically different story. Sobriety was hard for Andrew to maintain, and I think it's partly because every experience was slightly scarring him; Andrew was just too damn sensitive for the world.

In June 2009, Andrew overdosed, as aforementioned—this book is meant to be a glimpse at who he was—who I *was*, before we got here.

I evaluated our experiences in the context of a case-study approach.

Through my reminiscing in writing this book, I have found that all of life is connected whether people choose to recognize it or not, but often, it's impossible to see that interconnectivity while still being immersed within the web of it.

Hindsight isn't just a bias, it's the answers to questions you couldn't answer then.

This book is the direct result of my upbringing.

CANDLES NEED AIR TO BURN

Quite obviously, I was not a precocious learner—I barely kept up and yet I somehow seemed to be learning more than those around me despite how it appeared.

For all that I may have achieved so far in my life, remember that I also had to work twice as hard as the average person to get there because I am dyslexic.

In a Campbell's condensed soup version (my book *Wisdom 23*), after I got held back at the conclusion of the academic year in third grade, I subsequently also struggled with every math class I have ever taken— to the extent that during high school, I repeated the **first semester** of U.S. History and Algebra II during my **second semester** of my junior year, while still taking the second semester of both classes.

As in, I took both semesters of both courses at the same time.

A month after Andrew died, I left for college and attended Northern Arizona University—only to finish my first year in a flaming pile of ashes and ruin—that I immediately retroactively withdrew from because I failed multiple classes, but hey, it's okay because the only "A" I got that entire year was in *Transition to College,* so I must know what I'm doing, clearly. Or maybe, that class was a silly requirement.

Obviously, my bad grades almost flunked me out of college and I got academically suspended—pending probation for extenuating circumstances. Again, a situation concocted out of my own doing and poor decision making. I was impulsive.

To say the least about the whole situation, I was little unhinged emotionally at the time, and that contributed significantly to my erratic performance.

I wasn't angry or upset at anyone about Andrews death, but the grief was consuming me and **I started writing compulsively to cope**.

When I say "compulsively," I mean stacks of paper, hours on end rewriting the same poem over and over and over and over, but also changing it one word at a time during each rewrite. I kept writing until I couldn't hear the words anymore. I published one book, then another, and then another...

I appealed my suspension/probation at NAU over the summer of 2010 prior to starting my sophomore year. I met with someone from NAU's psychiatry department who was to evaluate my dedication to receiving a potential "second chance;" I got reinstated as a full-time student—no probation at the conclusion of the meeting.

I then continued on for another year at NAU—as a psychology major and petitioning for upper-level psych courses in the process, which I took and succeeded in by earning 3.0+GPA for back-to-back semesters leading into the summer. In my mind, I had redeemed myself of the challenge that I initially failed. I didn't have to stay there necessarily, but I had to "finish it."

However, I wasn't done quite yet. To top it off, I took a single, six-week summer school class in statistical psychology that I passed successfully—a math class that I actually passed.

To ensure my success, I met with the professor ahead of enrolling and explained my woes with mathematics; he assured me we'd get through the requirement together.

At the end of the course and after the final (he requested we hang out until everyone finished), he looks around the room and says,

"This has been great—went by so fast. It was wonderful getting to know each and every one of you, and I look forward to seeing you all in a class of mine next semester," and I was planning to take his course too, but then he turns to me as he is still addressing the class, "But for those of you with an IQ over 140, you really shouldn't be here at all—there's nothing for you, you're in the wrong place—so I hope that I do not see *you* again."

Most everyone in the room seemed puzzled by his departing statement, myself included, and then a petite female voice way off to the side of the room from a girl name Barbara asked "how do you know if you're IQ is over 140?"

The professor says with a smile, "you can get tested for it formally—I used to do that as a part of my profession for a long while, but it's a little more obvious when there's just one person asking all the questions and nobody has the answers yet" then he turns to me and winks.

Instantaneously, we all got up and left, but I *really* left.

I came back home to California as soon as the course grade for statistical psychology was posted the next day.

From my perspective, I suddenly saw where my life was going and I realized that I wanted no part of it; that professor had opened my eyes: the inevitable outcome of eventually graduating from NAU was not where I wanted my life to be. Because of my struggle, I had developed imposter syndrome regarding my intelligence—I still have it. So, instead of methodically planning a transition like most normal people, I changed everything all at once and ran (drove) home in a very characteristic-of-me way.

When I returned home, it was no Joseph Campbell hero's return.

The first thing that I did once I returned home was signing-up for classes at Saddleback Community college—which coincidentally, started that next morning. At the conclusion of that semester, I had gloriously failed two of four classes.

What the hell is wrong with me, right?

Trust me, I wondered it frequently.

The two courses that I failed were in psychology – and the classes I passed were art, of course.

Both parents referred to such courses as "basket weaving," or a waste of time and money. I did not think that Drawing Fundamentals or taking Color Theory was a "waste of time." It seemed like a valuable thing to learn, for me at least, and here was this teacher with years of experience ready to tell me how—I failed to see their problem with it.

I wanted to do some art.

Apparently that was like speaking blasphemy to my parents.

So when I finally became "serious" a semester later, I had a lot of damage control to do academically. My transcripts were all over the place, not just with grades but subjects and difficulty. There were many strange instances of failing a "foundational" prerequisite course that I petitioned to have taken concurrently with an upper division successor class, which I aced.

I retook those classes that I had failed twice already at Saddleback (again) for a passing grade, and when I paid attention, it was surprisingly easy for me. Go figure, right? I even friended my professors on Facebook I enjoyed the course so much. We still stay in touch.

My only thoughts: "Why the hell was I not doing it this way in the beginning?!" I had only myself to blame for that.

THE REAL RETURN

After I was admitted to Chapman University on probation for Fall 2013, which came after an initial rejection for the spring 2013 term, (and a successful appeal for fall), I earned a 3.8 GPA during my first semester at Chapman and subsequently joined two honors societies.

I achieved a 4.0 the semester after—my first 4.0 GPA *ever*—at the most difficult school I had ever attended.

What in the world?

Apparently, I was the one holding myself back the entire time.

In this instance, I wanted to *prove* to Chapman's administration that I belonged there, because I did belong there.

Years earlier, Andrew had been accepted to attend Chapman but my father wouldn't let him enroll and then he meandered around and got into drugs. Therefore, I needed to be accepted and attend in his honor– don't know *why* I felt that I need to do that, but who cares? It motivated me enough to do the things I'd been avoiding until then. Chapman couldn't stop me:

I *will* be excellent. I will *achieve.*

Once I have truly made up my mind, I challenge anyone brave enough to stand in my way as I come charging by, waves of motivational momentum rippling off the wake of my defiant determination to achieve.

While attending Chapman, I made it my mission to saturate their campus with my undeniable presence to spite the initial rejection I received. Because why not?

I got myself published in *Chapman Magazine,* several literary journals, had my own art gallery for three and a half months in Chapman's Leatherby Library, and a watercolor painting of mine also made the cover of *Calliope: Art & Literary Magazine*. Additionally, I published six books during my career there–four of which were released on the same day in December in four different genres–and I did it for no other reason than to have done it; a professor of mine had said during lecture that it was hard for authors to "cross genres" because the "styles change so much."

Then, during my second and final year as an undergraduate at Chapman, I petitioned for several independent study courses (for pace reasons) and got them added, so then of course I petitioned to double-overload my schedule in my last semester in order to graduate with the class of 2015—which is when all of my friends would be graduating.

I succeeded.

Full-time status is 12 credits (four courses) and I took 24 credits (eight courses; mostly literary classes); my GPA was a 3.5 that last semester. I had to read 47 novels across those eight classes. Never, ever do that. I highly un-recommend that specific strategy.

If you take away nothing else from reading my story, remember this:

The girl who kept excelling and achieving at the most difficult school she'd ever attended is the same one who failed much easier courses at way easier schools—so what does that really say about me and my ability to achieve? Or the educational system for that matter? Or my ability to cope with dyslexia?

I didn't suddenly get "smarter" and the classes certainly were not any easier. "What happened" is that I finally stopped getting in my own way and let myself happen.

I consciously changed my perspective of *why* I needed to succeed, and everything else kind of followed.

It took me seven years to get my undergraduate degree completed and I changed my major three times. Then, to confuse every academic statistic further, it took me exactly **four semesters** (two years) to earn my Master of Fine Arts degree from Chapman University, which I was awarded in May 2017 with honors. I also published another two books while in graduate school; one of those became my thesis—which is a full-length novel, because I'd never hand-in a half-baked cake and call it a party, even though the thesis requirement was only half a book with an outline for the rest. Call me an overachiever; that would almost be ironic, wouldn't it?

So, while I was in college pursuing both degrees, I managed to write and publish those 14 books (nine of which contain over eight hundred and fifty poems) on my own, while also creating over two hundred original works of art.

It's weird, right?

Before I graduated and lost Andrew, I'd never imagine myself capable of such a feat—publishing a lone book, and now look what I've done.

So what made me continue academically—why keep trying if I failed?

Well, that's very simple; I didn't "fail."

I learned a new way of how not to do something if I want a specific result. That is process of elimination through reverse engineering; two skills that I'm given the opportunity to improve through this circumstance or situation; that's not failure.

Maybe I like the challenge—maybe I needed it?

That's it.

I'm a rebel; I enjoy proving people wrong—

Please, underestimate me, tell me it's impossible—tell me all about how it's just not plausible or possible, and cannot be done. It would bring me no greater joy than to hear someone denounce my ability---the statement like kerosene to my motivational flames; go ahead, fan me with your doubt, ignite me, and then watch me get high off the success of showing you one of the many ways it can apparently be done.

It took years to figure out that I was creating all the problems (as a form of savior-self-sabotage) for myself, maybe to solve because the issues I didn't have were already solved—and where's the fun in that?

Don't get me wrong—my family's life was in no way "easy" and just like most families, we had our dysfunction that we made functional.

However, for my success, maybe I needed to have that of feeling of "being the underdog" in order to access that vast reservoir of unknown strength within me that enables me to achieve all that which felt previously unconquerable.

Am I destined forever to feel like a square peg shoved out through the other side of a round hole that couldn't hold me—prolific. Maybe what I am doesn't quite have a name yet. Maybe it doesn't need a label.

Several years ago, when I first wrote *Wisdom 23,* (when I was 23 years old), I included a similar perspective of my childhood and memorable instances of my college experiences—and subsequent achievements.

For those who read the book, some of my current narrative probably felt similar in some instances, but also it may have felt as though you were looking at things through a different lens—everything might've seem slightly warped, like a kaleidoscope of memories untangled into a mosaic of glass hanging free—the light shining through its shingles creating a coherent image. I hope it was coherent.

For those who didn't read that other book, don't worry. You're already caught up.

Until recently, I had not seriously considered the long-term effect of my "childhood narrative," and the impact that it would necessarily have upon my "adult life" as a whole—or how the perception of my upbringing had positively and negatively contributed to becoming the person I am today:

I am the Creative Director of my own company, Meeüz (pronounced "mewz") which produces content for medical device companies and those in the related industries. Additionally, and unrelated to MedTech, Meeüz publishes books under its own nom de plume, Purple Heifer Publishing; books vary in authorship and range in genre. Because why not?

However, let's be clear...

Whether I ever hold another executive position again or never write another book or word of poetry for the public to consume, I've already far exceeded any expectation anyone ever initially had of me and that is my life's greatest accomplishment. I'm like a racehorse running victory laps around the other horses after winning the Belmont, taking my own version of the famed Triple Crown title.

Is it still exciting?

Sure, success is exciting, but it likely matters a bit more if you see it for yourself, in person—or if you're the person succeeding.

And maybe in that moment is when it matters the most.

And if I do continue to achieve, to write, to publish, then I am only contributing to the fact that I broke out of a broken educational system that repeatedly failed me. Then I learned how to manipulate it for my success so that I could say with full knowledge and comprehension:

We expect the wrong things from students and fail to imbue them with critical thought processes that enable innovation and free-minded thinking for a higher-age culture.

3
Childhood Memories

What's your first memory—are there people there, can you name them? How old are you; do you even know where you are?

Imagine being able to recall those moments in perfect detail; all the triumphs and setbacks replayed—a screening of your earliest years, just for you.

Would you see your current career inside your childhood self, or did you make yourself into the person you are today?

If you had the opportunity, would you do it all over again the same way or would you change things?

CONSUELO AND GAMBIT

Bali, Indonesia—I'm moving towards breathing water—a tide coming and going, like the wind through the trees but there were no trees and I felt no wind except for a gentle breeze. Hands caught my falling strides towards the shore—Consuelo, my nanny from Manila, picked me up and carried me to the water; I was eighteen months old at the time. My family lived in Tokyo, Japan for the first two and half years of my life, and we frequently visited Asian countries near Japan for vacations.

Before Consuelo, my mom had a local Japanese caretaker watch Andrew and me while she went out. One seemingly benign day, she went out to the grocery store. When she returned, I was nowhere to be found.

We lived on the fifth story of an apartment complex and the balcony door was open. Yes, the eighteen-month old baby crawled out onto the balcony. My mother couldn't even freak out on the Japanese lady yet, her maternal instincts driving her outside first and very quietly, she walked to the edge of the balcony to where a drainage hole was located and looked over with a heavy heart. I had crawled through the hole and out onto the very thin beam that connected our balcony to that of our neighbor—it's a twenty-foot stretch. I was half-way across and out of reach from my mother's desperate attempts to grab me. There's a clear, unobstructed drop five stories to the pavement below me.

"Alexa, sweetie, Alexa come to mommy."

She repeated softly in a gentle, loving way, "I didn't want to scare you, I was worried you might fall. It was the scariest moment of my entire life. I don't like to talk about it."

I guess I started scooching backwards towards my mother and "soon as I could grab your little legs I picked you up" she recounts. It's a miracle I didn't fall to my very infantile death. After that episode of Alexa-challenges-death, my mother hired Consuelo. Her job was to supervise Andrew and I. Consuelo is an angel; I've never met a more patient, kind, and giving person than her. The values of her home culture are precious and endearing character traits.

After Japan, most of which I do not remember, my father transferred companies from Baxter to SciMed in Plymouth, Minnesota; his climb up the corporate ladder began.

Made Genius

~

Out in the snow—cold. I want to be inside but its so far and the sky is getting dark. Where is everyone—why am I out here, in the cold? What if I'm stuck out here forever? It won't be forever but it feels like forever. Is it dark because it's snowing or because it's getting late? I don't understand the concept of time. What if I can't make it up the hill; I've already tried twice and I can't get up it. The snow is too deep and I'm too small.

Suddenly I see something zigzagging towards me—reddish in color, it's Gambit, Andrew's dumb golden retriever! We sent him to duck hunting school and "he got stuck on the island. He never swam to shore—they had to go out and rescue him after three days." Untrainable—I grabbed onto Gambit's collar and he walked me up the hill and to the front door where Consuelo was standing. Her hands picked me up out of the snow and out of my soaked boots. I wore the wrong boots for the snow. She warned me, "your boots will wet in the snow." I didn't understand, partly because I just didn't understand that some materials were not water-resistant; I was three but I'll be damned if I didn't have my autonomy. So I protested and wore the boots I wanted to wear out into the snow, and she let me go so I'd learn.

Did Gambit come to rescue me intentionally? Probably not, he likely just needed to go outside and then got distracted by the tiny human struggling and he was a convenient height to use as a crutch—or he saved me. You can believe whichever you'd like; I like to think that latter.

That's my only memory of Gambit because when we left the snowy winters of Minnesota for the snowy, less-cold winters of Massachusetts, Gambit couldn't come. And no, my family didn't leave him at a shelter; we found him a home with some good family friends—The Boltons. (Note that I am pluralizing their name, not adding an unnecessary, possessive apostrophe (I'M JUST SAYING).

I don't remember the members of the Bolton family individually, because in my mind The Boltons are a single entity; families get pluralized and become a thing in my mind. We actually visited Gambit twice because the first time was right before we moved, and the second time we were in the area for a family reunion, and we would've gone again a third time a few years later— but by that time, it had been so long that he just wasn't around anymore, but he had a good life.

It's just sad that Andrew nor I could really be part of it because we were just too young to take care of an untrainable dog.

The first time that we visited Gambit, he jumped in my Dad's jaguar because he thought he was coming home, but he wasn't, and that was really kind of sad for all of us also. In fact, I obsessed about getting a pet—I got a ragdoll cat, whom I named Dakota not long after returning home.

The next and last time that we saw Gambit, I don't think he recognized Andrew and I the same way—we were bigger, not the tiny kids that he remembered us as.

The Boltons told us during that the reason Gambit seemed quiet and obedient now was because their other dog had just died by drowning, and Gambit was depressed.

At the time, I think I was maybe eight or nine; the next time I asked about Gambit when I was older, my mother informed me that he was gone.

During that same time for me in Andrew's life, he was preoccupied with asking my dad to tell him about "the deadliest diseases of the world—and don't tell me about AIDS because I already know about that one" he said affirmatively.

Insatiably curious, skeptical, and creative; his mind was a misunderstood masterpiece. My father couldn't answer Andrew's questions then nor now, as he would need the background of a PhD to compete with his son.

In lieu of familial-sourced cognitive stimulation, Andrew began reading books for those answers. He consumed book after book voraciously; "he was a machine," my father recounts. By eleven, Andrew had read Dante's Inferno, *East of Eden*, *The Great Gatsby;* all of the *Goosebumps* series by R.L. Stein, H.P. Lovecraft, the *Left Behind series*, as well as *Dune*. He also read most of the works from C.S. Lewis, Vonnegut, and Hemmingway. Andrew pretty much engulfed anything you'd put in front of him and he would immediately develop a very strong opinion about it. He took on *War and Peace*, *Gulliver's Travels* (one of his favorites), *Ulysses, Brave New World, As I Lay Dying, 1984, Fahrenheit 451, Anasi Boys, Catch-22*, Joseph Campbell's *The Hero's Journey*—all before he ever entered high school.

Later, and during his sophomore year in high school at Sage Hill, Andrew read a book by Maya Angelou that he hated so much, that he felt compelled to burn the words out of his mind, by literally burning the book. After much persistence and debating, my mother finally allowed him a controlled effigy burning as the conflagrator.

That "controlled" conflagration had been intentionally guided to become a small wall of feisty flames that blocked the street—which didn't really matter in actuality since we lived in a private neighborhood, and no one else was coming down that street, but it was a bit much. I just remember Andrew laughing manically as the book burned—perhaps a tad dramatic. However, it was a fairly harmlessx albeit a thermodynamically potent form of self-expression.

FIRST FRIENDS

I met my first best friend in Minnesota too—Rachel Spence. My mother comes up to me one day,

"Do you remember the girl that lives across the street?"

"Not really."

"She broke her arm the other day."

"How?"

Rachel had apparently fallen (or more literally "bounced") out of her open bedroom window while jumping on her bed—which was on the second floor of her house; she consequently broke her arm on the landing. After explaining that's what happens when kids jump on their bed, my mother continued to teach me the social skills I clearly lacked.

"You should go over and see her."

"Why?"

"It might make her feel better."

"Okay."

The concept of spending time with people to comfort them was lost on me.

Rachel's right arm was in a maroon sling when we were introduced again. This time I would remember her and would go over to her house nearly every day if she wasn't already at mine. I was incredibly shy around new people and would only communicate with those whom I knew well, otherwise I was quiet, silent—like a little mouse.

Andrew and Alexa at ages 6 and 3

I'm not really sure how or why, but while we were still living in Minnesota, Andrew and his friend Ben found a meteorite. For some reason, Andrew thought that it would be "really interesting" to put the meteorite in the microwave for two minutes. I thought it was going to end poorly.

"I don't think you should do that."

"I'm not doing anything wrong."

"Yes you are."

"Shut up, no I'm not."

"I'm telling mom."

"Mom's not here."

"I'm telling Consuelo."

"Consuelo is napping."

"You're going to break the microwave."

"No I'm not."

"Yes you are."

"Shut up. Why are you still here?"

Made Genius

Andrew pressed start. Ben lived next door and was familiar with how Andrew and I interacted, which was argumentatively. Fifteen seconds into the two-minute count down, the rock began to spark bright colors like little electric eels lunging out in random directions. Every time one of the sparks made contact with the rock or frame of the microwave, there was a "popping" sound. Andrew had put the meteorite in the microwave on a paper towel thinking he'd be able to use that to pull it out after. Why he thought microwaving a rock was a good idea to begin with is beyond me.

"That sounds bad" I say knowing full-well that is not how things should sound in a microwave.

"Shut up" Andrew snaps.

"What's happening?" Ben asks.

"I don't know, something is exploding " Andrew starts to say as I interrupt, "—He's breaking the microwave."

"What's exploding?" Ben asks..

"I'm not sure, it must be electromagnetic—this is awesome" Andrew says, enamored by the green sparks flying off the rock.

"There's smoke" I say flatly.

"Shut up—go away"

"There's a lot of smoke. I think it's going to catch on fire" I say while watching the napkin beneath the object already catching on fire.

"Shut up—you don't know what you're talking about."

"Okay. Fire—The paper towel is on fire" I say flatly again.

"What?" Ben asks since he can't see.

"Stop the microwave!" Andrew screams at me.

"Turn on the sink!" Ben exclaims.

"I told you."

"I didn't break the microwave idiot" Andrew says with annoyance.

"You started a fire" I say.

"That's not breaking the microwave" he clarifies.

"It's fire" I contest.

"Yes, Man's greatest invention—Mom will never know." Andrew says patronizingly.

"I'm telling her when she gets home."

"No you're not. You have no proof. She will never believe you."

Consuelo walked into the kitchen and glares at Andrew, who is holding a meteorite with oven-mitts; the meteorite is steaming. The microwave door is still open, and Ben pushed it shut as Consuelo shifted her glance to me.

"What's going on here?" Consuelo asks,

"Andrew started a fire."

"What—Where?" she asks.

"It's gone now."

"Andrew did you start a fire?" She asks him.

"Technically it was electricity" he says matter-of-factly.

"Don't do it again" her words sounding firmer now.

"Okay."

"That's it?" I ask.

"Stop tattling on your brother." And then she walked away.

"Why do I get in trouble when you do something wrong?" I say to myself.

"Because I'm smarter than you"

"..."

4

FIRST GRADE

First grade at Deerfield Elementary in Massachusetts, I had Miss Tadisco—my friends and I even participated in her wedding when she became Mrs. Hardy. I didn't know exactly what was happening at the time or why my teacher's name had to change, but I was happy to be part of that really fun party. My teacher looked beautiful—I hadn't seen anyone prettier than her that day. My mom did my hair really nice for the wedding and my best friend Patrick was going to be my fake date. He and I hung out and played power rangers together.

I didn't understand Mrs. Hardy's class. First, it was the projector. All year I sat copying her words onto my paper and then one day she says to the class, "Alright everyone, stop trying to write like me. I want you to write with your own style." We were supposed to be writing like her?! I felt so annoyed and angry. Apparently, it was in the written instructions that I couldn't read. I did a lot of guessing with what I was intended to do for an assignment. Sometimes I was right, most times I was very, very wrong. We were supposed to do math using these green square tiles made of plastic; they were maybe about an inch long on each side and very flat. There were yellow ones too, but they "meant" something different than the green tiles. Some of the green tiles were in halves, like triangles, and the right arrangement of two made them into squares again. There were sheets with empty tile spaces and we were supposed to answer our math questions by filling in the spaces with the tiles and then removing the tiles and coloring them in. I didn't understand the point of that when I saw the end result, so I didn't use the tiles and I made really pretty designs inside the squares instead. After all, each answer created a sort of design with the tiles. Was I not supposed to create my own? That was not the intention of the assignment and I was labeled a dysfunctional learner. I should've been brave and asked questions—but my educators should've known better and asked me theirs.

My friends helped me cheat when it came to reading and spelling. I only a had a few friends—girl scouts from my troop, and they were sensitive to my illiteracy. The other kids were mean and bullied me for it. I couldn't stand to be humiliated—they were asking me to spell things that they knew I'd misspell, just to laugh at the fact I couldn't do it. I felt so stupid. I hated myself for it. I would go home at night and cry over my homework desperately trying to decode the words on the page to no avail. Sometimes Andrew would swing by and give me the answers, but I couldn't count on that. Usually he was preoccupied with playing games on the computer or reading a book, and he hated to be disturbed while he read.

5
MYSTERIES OF MASSACHUSETTS

HALE RESERVATION

 When Andrew and I moved to Westwood, Massachusetts in 1994, we lived in an apartment for almost a year while our mother designed and built our house from the ground up. Consuelo moved with us again; first from Tokyo, Japan to Plymouth, Minnesota—then again to Westwood. This is also when my mother became pregnant with Somer.

The lot my parents bought for our new house would later become a seven-year long law suit regarding the nature of the sediment the lot contained—it was full of rocks. Literal, giant boulders blanketed the entire lot, forcing the foundation to be built lower which also cost more money to do, and it was not disclosed in the initial purchase agreement—hence the law suit that ensued.

The lot backed a forest at a junction between the Charles River Conservation Land, Hale Reservation, and the Noanet Woodlands; in it were mysterious, magical things that cannot be explained, even until this day. About twenty feet into the woods from our yard was the beginning of a stone wall—stacked stones about two feet high, and it curved its way through the forest, winding around trees and bordering natural landmarks. The stone wall was built by the Native Americans, one side of the wall was the reservation; the other side was the burial grounds—sacred land.

I still couldn't read yet, but I could listen, and I absorbed everything anyone said about the forest, especially Andrew, since he knew so much. He talked to me about science and nature; I was fascinated. Our landscaper John said that he found "giant snapping turtles down at the creek, about a mile or two into the woods" and they were so large "you could've ridden them." I tried to imagine a turtle that large in my little child mind. I couldn't. John was a cool guy; he made the yard look amazing and he let Andrew drive the bobcat that he had at our house for intense landscaping. My mom voiced some concern at first, but John reassured her that "he's in a cage, he'll be fine." Andrew was eight. Eight. John let Andrew drive the bobcat at eight years old because the yard was getting torn up anyway, so what would be the harm? Not like he was going to destroy anything John wasn't going to destroy on his own. I had no such desires to participate.

I was out exploring and spying on the neighbors. I did that regularly, spying on the neighbors I mean. Maybe some people would see that as some kind of invasion of privacy, and it totally was but I had no sense of it. I had secret paths mapped out that could get me from one house to then next. I chronicled my journeys in my own backwards language and hand-drawn pictures that I kept in a special notebook. I studied people, watched them interact and talk. I was so frustrated with school that I escaped into my own fantasyland that was more exciting, adventurous—reading didn't matter and those strict rules I made myself follow didn't apply. My quest was to learn by experience. Half-way down my street, Skyline Drive, where the hill began to steeply decline was one of my favorite places; it was just before the bus stop. This giant boulderish-rock[3] created a miniature hill next to the sidewalk; it was too steep to leisurely walk up—it had to be climbed. And I loved climbing things; I climbed everything. Trees, rocks, walls—yes walls, the walls of my house specifically.

My mom walked into her room one day as I just reached the top of the archway to her bathroom. At five, that was a good eight-foot climb and I was barely three feet tall; like a spider monkey, I just kind of shimmied my way up the archway with ease. I knew my feet had to be at a certain angle to stick, and I had to push hard enough with my arms so as not to fall and support my weight. The expression on my mom's face was priceless. She wasn't mad, confused, or shocked which was unexpected. She looked a little surprised but was smiling, amused almost.

"How did you get up there?"

---

[3] **boulderish-rock:** too large to be considered a "rock," yet lacks the qualities of a typical "boulder" shape; more monolithic by construction but not by human intent, it is naturally formed that way. One or more of the sides may appear flat, giving the boulderish-rock a slab-like appearance from one or more angles of one's perspective.

"Climbed."

"Can you get down?"

"Yeah, wanna see me climb back up?" I said enthusiastically.

"Sure."

I just released my arms and legs and plopped to the floor with a thud—that's when my mother made a strange face; I seemed un-phased by it, because I climbed back up and jumped down again excited to show my mother my new trick.

I had a favorite tree in our yard that I liked to climb. My mom warned me about climbing thin branches, and hoisting myself up on weaker branches that might not be able to support my weight—or not for very long if they seemed stable. I remember breaking a tiny tree's branch out in the front yard, I felt so guilty about it but never said anything. Instead I would visit the tree every day and talked to it—I thought if I spent time with it like I did with Rachel, it might make the tree feel better. I was a kid—I didn't know trees don't have feelings the same way people do. But in any case, it didn't slow me down; if I couldn't get up into to a big tall tree, I'd climb a smaller one and leap over. I think my haphazard approach to getting down is what worried my mother. Shortly after this little discovery, I was enrolled in gymnastics because my mom figured I'd probably enjoy it.

One day, not long after the archway incident, I got it in my head that I could jump from the catwalk and land safely on the ground below, which happened to be wood flooring and is very hard—not like carpet. I needed to be sure that I could do it though, so I decided to do a test-trial.

I climbed up the steps of the stairs on the wrong side of the railing; then I began my experiment by jumping off each step just one step higher each time, and landing on the wood floor below. At the sixth step I felt the sting from landing on the wood as the shock shot up my feet, ankles, and lower legs, stopping at my knees... I'd never experienced such a sensation—I'd later identify that strange sensation as pain, but at the time it was a curious feeling. So being the scientific child I was, I repeated the process and documented the experience of landing and feeling the sting with each step that I climbed. I kind of liked it at first—or it didn't necessarily "bother" me—the pain I mean. It was just odd; I have an incredibly high pain threshold and a high tolerance too. I was fearless. After I leapt from the tenth step the sting was different and I fell to my knees. I shook out my legs as I tried to walk it off. They felt "silly," like I was trying to walk with noodle-legs on Jell-O. I didn't climb as high on my next trial, I only climbed up to step nine. Nine didn't hurt like ten did. Nine was my limit. I elected not to leap from the catwalk because nine was significantly lower than the top, which was fifteen steps. A few years later, Somer pushed Dakota, my cat, from the catwalk. He broke his hip on the landing and had to be confined to our laundry room for weeks while he recovered. I thought back to how I once considered jumping off the catwalk—I felt pleased with my decision not to jump off of it, and was proud of my methodology for testing whether I could. However, it seems that fate wouldn't approve. One way or another, it seems I'd have to arrive at an inevitable outcome: injury.

Gymnastics didn't last long—I saw everyone jumping off one of the high-rise trampolines and I thought they were jumping to the ground, but they weren't. There was a ledge that led to the mid-level trampoline and that's where everyone was congregating. So, when I jumped after them, I missed the ledge and landed on the outside of both my ankles; it was over a twelve-foot drop, probably close to fifteen feet because nobody ever jumped all the way down. Ever. I screamed out in pain—pain. That was the sting, but this was so much worse. It all made sense in that instance. I ruined the ligaments in my ankles from that day forward, and anytime I ran or moved awkwardly, I'd roll one, the other, or both ankles simultaneously. My days of leaping from high places were over. I could still climb, but no more jumping down. I was back to exploring the ground and all the little details I'd been missing out on.

In my own backyard I found an endangered species—the Lady Slipper flower; there were hundreds of them near the right side of our property. They were kind of in our backyard, down below hill and just behind the custom play structure that my mom had built for us. The flowers bloomed during the spring through the summer in pink and white; the stem dipped downward near the top and held the flower and its petals like a chandelier above the ground—it looked just like a slipper and was identical to the picture that I was referencing from Andrew's book that I had "borrowed." I couldn't read the words at all, but I could understand some of the "word-shapes" and all of the pictures, of course; At five years old, I was certain that it was the most beautiful thing I'd ever seen; it seemed so fragile. I would sit in the woods for hours just staring at the flowers. I knew it was "illegal" to pick or disturb them, and I didn't know exactly what illegal "meant," aside from the fact that I shouldn't do it. So I didn't. I was very strict with myself regarding any rules, may they be life, school, or ones my parents made...Andrew, not so much. He liked to break them, test them, or prove them wrong—and he'd drag me into it if he could, but I resisted more often than not. Between the two of us, my mother deemed me the responsible one—maybe because I was a tad bossy but probably because Andrew was notoriously impulsive, and that was worse.

Impulse. Imagine Einstein's brain with the maturity of a young child; it's like intelligence on meth. Hyperactive, intelligent, and meticulous; Andrew knew how to have fun.

THE BEEHIVE

Our mother is highly allergic to bees. Both Andrew and I knew how to administer the epi-pen. My mom saw a bee in the basement, then another in the sill. I kept getting stung but wouldn't realize it until some part of me was swollen. That was concerning considering that our mother liked to be outside doing stuff in the garden or improving the house somehow. Andrew took it upon himself to protect our mother and destroy the hive.[4] While my mom was off doing something, Andrew got into cabinet below the kitchen sink. There, he collected the ingredients to make some kind of explosive. Not like fire-explosive, but like, shake-shake-shake, chemical-reaction explosive. Andrew got one of the tall "kid-cups" that he told me never to drink out of—because he likes to mix chemicals and they are the perfect height. So I didn't. I hated those cups.

Andrew helped me get dressed-up in the winter gear during the middle of the summertime. I put on the ski goggles, ski mask, a helmet, a scarf to cover my neck—no part of my skin was exposed. I'm seven. Andrew gives me my instructions.

"You need to move very quickly. Try not to shake the bottle at all until you're at the hive, then shake it, leave it, and run. Run really fast."

"Why do I have to do it?" He looked too excited. I don't trust that.

"Because I said so."

Andrew was smart. He wasn't worried about me getting blown up—he helped cover my skin so that I could get close enough to the hive without getting stung a hundred times. He of course didn't tell me why, I just did what he said and was left to figure it out. I went to the hive. I walked over there so that I wouldn't accidentally shake the contents. When I arrived at the hive, all I heard was buzzing and there were bees everywhere. I

---

[4] Do not destroy beehives. Bees are good, they pollinate a ton of fruit. In retrospect, we should've relocated them.

shook the bottle, left it and ran. There was an unexpected casualty of nature caught in the crossfire—the tree that the hive was mounted to suddenly got its seasons reversed: it thought fall was spring, and that the summer was actually winter. It died a year later and had to be chopped down. I made it out of the situation unscathed.

POTATO CANNONS AND LION FISH

Perhaps one of my favorite family friends are the Wetteraus, note that they're also an entity. They have three children: Elizabeth, Stephen, and Olivia; Stephen is the same age as Andrew, Olivia is a year ahead of me, and Elizabeth is older than both Andrew and I. Mark and Ginny are their parents and they bring the fun with them wherever they go. They had this big dog named Kojack and he liked to bark, which scared me. Kojak was an Australian Heeler. Then she got this little fluff-ball dog that she named Todd, and he was just hyper. I liked her cats better. She had a black one named Elvis and he had the softest, plushest fur of any cat I've ever known. But Elvis acted like a cat. The other lighter colored one was Raja, and he was friendlier. When the Wetteraus went on vacation for a week, my mom said she would go over and take care of the animals for Ginny.

So my mother takes me with her to go take care of the animals on the first night, and as we are standing at the garage door, she turns to me and says,

"I can't remember the garage code."
"What?"

"I forgot it."

"How are we going to get in?"

"I don't know."

It's 1998, there's no cellphones. I look at the side of the house and there's a door into the garage from the side. I walk over to it and try to open it, but it's locked.

"Do you have a key?"

"No."

She reaches down and pushes the doggy door open and then she stands back and looks at me.

"I think you could fit."

"What?"

"I think you could climb through the dog door. You're tiny enough."

"Wait, you want me to do this?"

"We have to feed their animals."

"But there's lady bugs all over the door."

"They're lady bugs—harmless. They're good luck."

"Says who?"

"Everyone. Now climb through the doggy door."

I resolve to do what my mother says. There are lady bugs all over the frame of the doggy door. I got my head through, then one shoulder at a time, my waist—I was stuck, no, I stopped. Kojack started barking at me. He heard me climbing through and came to defend his home.

"He's barking."

"You're fine."

"He's going to eat me!"

"He's not going to eat you."

"He's barking and getting closer. I'm scared."

"Don't be scared, tell him to stop."

"No! No Kojack!"

I rotated my hips slightly and slithered through. I got up and ran to the garage door opener on the wall like it was the buzzer to an imaginary timer on a game show. As soon as I hit it, I turned to Kojack and started petting him. He's not so scary after all. My mom and I went into the house where we had to feed the lion fish, which ate lettuce.

"They're very poisonous. If you touch one, you have to go to the hospital."

I watched my mother carefully place her hand in the tank and avoided the toxic lion fish. She clipped the lettuce to the inside of the glass—I assume it was meant to imitate some kind of seaweed. After she checked on all of the other animals, we left. I couldn't stop thinking about the lion fish. I had only seen them in aquariums—how cool was it that my mom's friend had one in her fish tank. I wondered why we didn't have more pets. I would've liked more pets.

~

Some months later, Andrew was bothering my dad about a potato cannon. Nobody really knew what sparked Andrew's sudden and intense interest in unconventional or otherwise obscure things, but they happened rather frequently and with equal intensity as the last fad-interest.

"I think Mark Wetterau made one with Stephen."

"Can we use it?"

"Probably. I'll call him and ask."

Of course Mark had already made one with Stephen—we weren't the first to come up with ridiculous avenues of entertainment. The Wetteraus and their brigade of all things awesome showed up with the potato cannon—a very unassuming piece of PVC pipe with a custom combustion chamber. It was a simple order of operations: Insert the potato, spray the cheap hairspray in the combustion chamber, aim the cannon, light the combustion chamber—brace for launch. Andrew was just a little too tiny to hold and aim the cannon on his own because of the kickback. So Mark, Stephen, and my dad "helped." We had a balcony on our deck that was the perfect launch zone for the potatoes; we had full range of the forest. The first potato hit the tree that Andrew murdered, the next one went off its mark and veered right beyond the Lady Slippers by the play structure; a potato exploded on the slide. After that, Mark made a minor adjustment and the potatoes kept going far out of sight into the forest, and they'd be unknown if not for their inevitable SMACK into a solid object. The smell of all those hair-sprayed spuds was awful, rancid—noxious; maybe Mark used rotten potatoes, I'm not sure.

Andrew wanted to build a potato cannon, but he quickly lost interest after shooting several potatoes; the new computer was more intriguing.

~

The computer was the most interesting thing Andrew had ever used and I know this because it's where he would spend all of his time if he wasn't reading. He used to write my stories for me too —I unfortunately couldn't write words yet because I couldn't read, so I dictated my wild stories to Andrew, who acted as my scribe. He typed out all my stories for me on the new computer and printed them with pride. He even put a report cover on them to make them look extra official. They were all of maybe five or six pages, with only a couple sentences on the page with a picture below, drawn of course by me, because I'm an artist too. I liked art and adventures; I turned into a confident, bold, daring person whenever I went out adventuring.

FIRES AND STEALTH BOMBERS

I was walking down the back stairs of my house in my favorite night gown, I'd just taken a shower but it was still light out. It was the summertime. That's when five fire trucks descended the hill in our driveway. Firemen came out of each fire truck and quickly went to work.
"Mom! Mom! There's a fire."
"What?"
"There's five fire trucks in the driveway" I exclaim.
"What are you—oh. That is extremely strange. There's no fire here."

We went outside to ask what was going on—a fire in the woods. Our neighbor, Mr. Stripack, has a daughter who was home visiting and happened to be looking at the forest through her telescope when she noticed smoke. After refocusing, she saw a fire and that's when she called 911. Our house, with it's incredibly long and spacious driveway, was the closest access point for crews to work from. Of course we were going to get out of the way, but we were also privy to first-hand action. Andrew excitedly picked anyone's brain who would let him. The crews worked into the night and I went to bed long before the fire was contained.

In the morning, the origin of the fire remained a mystery. There were no accelerants and no roadside access points—the firemen used our yard because it was the closest to the epicenter. After the fire was put out, a half charred semi-truck remained. How it got into the middle of the forest—that's another question. The next morning, my mother was awoken by the strange sounds of a radio emitting some type of static behind indecipherable babble. Andrew, who slept alone in the only room on the fourth floor, was awoken by the strange sounds too.

Usually, Andrew would come into my bed (and push me out of it) whenever he had nightmares or was woken up, but this time he ran to my mom's room to wake her up. He wanted to go investigate. My mom said "I swear to god the sounds were almost alien. There was nothing terrestrial about what we were hearing." And she was so spooked that she wouldn't let Andrew investigate. Some parents might try to discourage belief in alien life forms, or explain to their children why such things weren't to be feared since it might cause unnecessary anxiety—not my mother. Aliens are real and you should be afraid.

Several days after this incident, we coincidentally noticed a black non-squirrel—not a squirrel, more of a fisher-cat-like creature on the prowl.[5]
"What is that?"
"It's too big to be a squirrel, but it moves like one."

---

[5] **Fisher cat:** looks like a wild, slightly larger ferret or an animal that is related to the wild weasel; not actually a cat nor related to the feline family the same way prairie dogs are not actually canines.

The creature was quick, agile and daring. It was locked in a chase with a gray squirrel that was desperately trying to out run its new predator. The squirrel was a few trees ahead of the black non-squirrel of an unknown species. Their hot pursuit seemed predictable until the creature suddenly leaped through the air almost thirty feet and tackled the squirrel out of tree, taking it back into the forest and out of our range of sight.
"Well that was unexpected."
"I don't know of any animal that moves like that."
"Neither do I."

There are no squirrels in Westwood anymore, last that I heard.

~

Our family wasn't "churchy," so our Sundays consisted primarily of going to brunch and being hijacked by our mother to go "look at all the big houses." My mom liked to imagine how she would change each house that caught her fancy. She was always looking "for a house with really good bones." That was something not easy to find, a lot of houses are "garage houses," where "the focal point of the house is the garage." My mom despised those houses. She liked antiques, things with character. If it was unusual in an esoteric way, she liked that—if the unusualness was accidental and wonky, that was a turn off.

In any case, we had just finished having brunch in high-rise building in Boston when Andrew noticed a stealth bomber overhead, but only made mention of it when he could still see it following us still as we got onto the freeway.

"We are being followed" Andrew says without inflection.
"No we're not—by who" mother asks.
"The government"
"Not everything is a conspiracy theory."
"What's a conspiracy theory?" I ask.
"That's complicated. But there's definitely a stealth bomber following us" Andrew states with confidence.

That is when my mom, who was sitting in the passenger seat, starts looking around the sky—she saw the plane too. There it was, a stealth bomber; it's distinct triangular shape was hard to misidentify.

They flashed me their badges—I couldn't read but it looked official.

> "You can wait in here with the nice sofas. Kids aren't allowed on them because my mom said our body oils will ruin the fabric."

.[7] Strange as their appearance, it was, however, completely unrelated to the stealth bomber incident. During this time, my father drove a seven series BMW that was equipped with armor plating and bulletproof glass. When Andrew inquisitively asked about it, my dad's response seemed inadequate.

"It came like that."

"What do you mean?"

"I went to buy a car and this one just happened to have all the extra features."

Nobody believed him. Probably because it was all a bunch of bologna. Fire in the woods, the radio sounds, the stealth

---

[6] See below:

[7] This information has been redacted due to confidentiality and to ensure the public welfare of the community.

bomber ███████████████████[8]—my dad driving a bullet proof car. It seemed like some type of conspiracy, which made Andrew grow ever more confident that my dad was an analyst for the CIA. He wasn't, or so he says. But I was beginning to understand why Andrew thought a conspiracy was complicated.

There's a lot of compelling evidence that challenges the opposite of whatever my dad says, but I've seen my dad at work. His job is legit. But that doesn't stop the conspiracy theories from surfacing—all in good humor, of course.

NOBLES

In the same vein of the CIA family conspiracy theory comes the greatest summer camps of all summer camps: "Nobles," or the Noble and Greenough school, which is located in Dedham, Massachusetts. The school had a summer program that allowed its participants to have some unique experiences. There is a castle at the school, which in retrospect, would now resemble something very similar to Hogwarts in Harry Potter. The castle had secret passage ways and grand staircases; in one class, you had to scale the castle wall and then repel down the other side. Another class played hide and go seek, in the castle. There were tightrope wires high up in the trees and down low— kids were taught how to walk across them. They also had a rocket launching field for the bottle rockets too. Some of the other classes included lanyards, tie-dye, canoeing, dance, nature hike,

---

[8] See previous.

jewelry making, swimming, music, BB guns, archery, basket weaving, street hockey, field games and some others. They taught a lot of practical knowledge through an unassuming means.

Music class was a sing-along class equipped with sheet music to join in. All the music played were classics. I couldn't read any of it, but I learned lyrics quick and could anticipate them in time with the melody. Music was one of my favorite classes aside from lanyards and archery. I was good with BB guns but it scared me to be around the other kids who also had BB guns. They weren't very careful and I grew concerned that they might accidentally shoot me, so I took more archery classes instead. I was good at archery.

My canoeing classes were the best because I'd intentionally coax my fellow boat-mates into areas of the lake where we'd get incredibly stuck—or so they thought. Most boats had a counselor, but I was good enough that my crew didn't need to have one—instead they gave us a blow horn to call for help. So of course, I'd let us get stuck. I did this for two reasons: the first was that I got to have a closer look at the awesomeness of nature: the bugs, new plants—I watched the way algae swirled in the dark, almost black lake when I dragged my oar through the water. And since we weren't moving, I could actually look at it— though, it scared me a little to think of what might be below us; if we started to sink, then I might freak out. Getting stuck? I could unstick us, but it was kind of fun to watch the other kids freak out for a second or two before I pushed us off of the lake weeds. The second reason I'd get us stuck is to use the blow horn—

which I'd blow and then "miraculously" I'd unstick us. My overconfidence caused a lot of problems in that way. If I was proficient enough in the task that the situation required, then I would somehow cause chaos, if only for a moment. It was a total abuse of power, but at the time, I didn't see anything wrong with it—I was a kid. And because I acted innocently, no one was the wiser.

You'd think that all those exciting activities might deter me from taking the need for adventure out into the world—nope. I was the only one to get a field mouse trapped in my locker, and after screaming about its sudden appearance, I demanded its humane release into the wild. I did a complete 180 within a few seconds. One of the guys wanted to throw the mouse in a puddle and I remember threatening him in some way over the mouse, to which an adult counselor overtook the responsibility of the mouse's safe release. I even made a call to my mom about it because I was really upset that they might hurt the innocent mouse. It started to rain again and I got in an argument about tagging along, in the rain, to ensure the mouse's safety. Days where it rained weren't nearly as fun and I didn't always have to go to camp on those days, or sometimes we'd leave early. Somer was too young to join the camp, so it was just Andrew and I— except that he was placed with the older kids because he was older.

~

Despite all of these new skills we were learning, my mother didn't want us to go out into the world thinking of everyone as a friend. We had code words to verify whether or not someone we didn't know was actually picking us up, and my mom made sure that no matter where I was, I knew how to get home. The names of the streets don't matter, and neither did the numbers of the addresses so long as I knew where I was going. She even taught us that we can kick out the tail light of a car in the trunk if we were ever abducted. We were also taught how to psychologically disrupt the chain of events in an abduction, such as returning to the first scene, disappearing into a crowd of strangers, shadowing a family in a public place, and how to get help before you get caught by a kidnapper—things you don't think will ever happen to you are the types of things we were taught to maneuver. I suppose my mom was paranoid. Or maybe not, considering the types of shenanigans her offspring pulled. My mother would even have me direct her home from the grocery store to prove I knew the way at eight years old. I had to recite her phone number, the house number, and my dad's number too—I was constantly being asked to memorize information. I had to be told the same information repeatedly, but once I knew the information as my own, I couldn't ever forget it.

For example, there were two entrances to the neighborhood and one time, the bus driver drove me to my house because I fell asleep and he was worried I would be too groggy to navigate home. I woke up with my mom in front of me; quite frankly, it startled me. Another time on the bus, I fell asleep and woke up just as he was going out the back entrance of the neighborhood—my mom realized what I did when I missed the bus stop; she went out the other way and looped around so that she would intersect us at the back entrance. I was notorious for my chronic migraines and suddenly falling into a deep slumber. I needed my naps more than the average developing child.

There was a bully on that bus named Alex. He was younger than me and liked to spit chewed-up cheerios on people, and he harassed my beloved bus driver. I remember one especially brisk morning, Alex gets on and proceeds to spit cheerios into my eyes. I was so annoyed. It was one thing for the bigger kids to push me around, but not someone younger. That was unacceptable, and he was bullying the bus driver. I grabbed his cheerios and crushed them quickly. Then I opened the window next to him and let the cheerio smithereens get carried off by the passing wind. I handed Alex the empty bag.

"If you spit cheerios at me, or anyone else again, I'm not just going to tell your mom what you did, I'm going to tell mine."

Surprisingly, he sat back down and never bothered anyone again. By the end of the year, he was actually kind of a nice kid. He had friends even. They weren't on bus 3, but he had them. I was bullied a lot and didn't have very many friends, not on any other bus either—not yet at least.

~

Scout's Honor

I really wanted to join Boy Scouts because Andrew was in it and he was telling me about all the really cool things they were doing and learning. And they got to play with knives—I liked knives. My mom told me that they had girl scouts for girls, which was essentially like the "girl version" of boy scouts—it wasn't in actuality, but it had the same idea.

"I want a knife. Will they teach me to use one?"

"Yes."

"Fine."

First, the gave me a paper knife. A paper pocket knife. It was absolutely useless. I felt so patronized. The only purpose it had actually been designed for was to teach kids how to "properly pull out the blade into a fixed position" without cutting themselves. Too easy. I was sitting in front of a watermelon feeling really upset about this whole knife debacle, when a woman point-blank hands me a butcher knife.

"You know how to use that?"

"Yep."

"Okay, cut the watermelon for us."

She walked away, but no sooner than she left did my mom come over.

"Put that knife down!"

"No."

"No?"

"No. The lady gave it to me. Said cut the 'melon."

"You're going to hurt yourself."

"No I'm not."

It was illogical to wrestle a knife away from me—that could go poorly rather quick. I saw this instance as my moment to prove that I knew what I was doing. I rocked the knife back at an angle and punctured the rind; I put my other hand on the other end of the blade, and then I pushed down with all my strength. I cut it in half, but it was absolutely exhausting to do. I had to push down hard, like really hard. I lost interest almost immediately. But, when I went to visit my grandfather that summer, he gave me one of his special pocket knives. The blade wasn't even close to sharp, but it was tiny, discreet, and the handle was made of pearl. It was a beautiful knife—that was its purpose.

~

THE EXPLORER

My parents were good to me—my dad frequently took business trips and although I rarely saw him, he always tried to make up for it.

In the beginning, while I was still young, he would bring back items from the places he traveled to as he told a story. One time Andrew asked for a Harp seal, "It squirmed away from me at security—I chased it," my father gleefully told my brother, "but it was just too quick. He probably wouldn't have liked the plane very much anyway." And then my dad handed Andrew a stuffed seal and said that "this seal is an exact replica of the seal that got away." I'm sure he knew my dad wasn't serious and it didn't matter anyway. Andrew named the seal "Sealy" and he slept with it every night after that.

Our Christmases were extravagant; parties for the adults and a giant tree and presents for the children. It was a twenty-five-foot tree, such a big tree; we had the house for it. I could count on getting almost anything I wanted for Christmas from Santa, but he would purposely not get me something I really wanted, but I'd also get something I did want as well. I constructed my Christmas lists masterfully. Why does this matter? My father believed that I shouldn't get what I wanted, that life doesn't offer free hand-outs, so Santa shouldn't give them either.

My mother wanted me to enjoy my childhood, to get the most out of everything that she never could—to give me a life that she wished she could've had. What was so wrong with that? Well, my father would likely say, life doesn't work like that. Maybe he was right, or maybe he was just pessimistic. How did he get to where he was? It wasn't just hard work, he got lucky too. And he got lucky often. It happened so often that the two could even be confused. I grew into a teenager that had gotten what she wanted, so much that she never wanted anything except for she loved—her passion. My passion is what drives me, still drives me, but we will get to more of that later.

~

SMOKY MOUNTAINS

Tennessee is home to the famous Smokey Mountains—a place where the fog can get so thick, the mountains look smoky. We were taking the ordinary freeway route when some kind of alert flashed on the side of the road—up ahead rocks and boulders had fallen; the rockslide made the roads impassable. Succeeding signs alerted drivers of detours and alternate paths, but my mom kept the minivan at a steady 70 mph as we headed for a stoned wall, get it?

When we arrived at the pile of boulders in the middle of the freeway, it was only at that moment with such compelling evidence that my mother finally accepted the road was blocked. A new problem manifested as well: we couldn't turn around. Seven other cars followed us off the nearest ramp to a white-water river rafting loading zone. Hundreds of people were getting geared up to go down the most ferocious looking river I'd ever seen. We asked someone of authority where to go—they said "follow the road."

Only three cars followed now, I assume they were river-rafters. After going through some wooded area, we reached a really vast expanse of wilderness with the narrow dirt road passing right by a quaint cabin. An old man rocked along in his rocking chair smoking a pipe, waiting for us to pass. We didn't pass. My mother wanted "directions through the mountains" from "somebody who knew the land." Andrew sighed discontentedly, as he began a barrage of witticisms that combated her immediate intent.

"There's only one road—you probably just take it the next town."

"We don't know that, the road could split or loop—I don't want to get lost up there for hours—especially in the dark. I hate driving at night."

"This is the main road. It's dirt. It goes through" Andrew says.

"Do you have a map?" My mom says looking over at Andrew, no map in hand.

"Actually, yes, and it goes through."

"You're full of baloney" my mother says.

We pull up to the man's house since it's literally a few feet from the dirt road. He doesn't get up.

"Hey, do you know how to get through the mountains?"

"For a twenty I can remember the way" the old man says.

"Okay."

My mom hands him the money through the window—he got up to get the money; he's clearly financially motivated.

"Ya' see this here road—the one 'yer on?" he says with an accent I couldn't place.

"Yeah?"

"'Yer gonna wanna take this road into the forest."

"Okay..."

"And that's it."

"Take this road into the forest?"

"Yep. Ya' can't mess that one up."

"So we just follow this road?"

"Yessm."

Andrew is hysterical in laughter. It wasn't that funny, really it wasn't but I guess for Andrew, it was the goddamn funniest thing to happen all day.

"Calm down."

"Why? You just paid twenty dollars to hear what I already told you."

"I wanted to be sure."

"I was."

"Whatever. We will just have to rough it. The minivan can probably make it."

"I told you we should've rented the jeep."

"No—they're dangerous."

Because driving into the Smoky Mountains of Tennessee in a minivan on a dirt road under the guidance of an old man smoking out of his corncob pipe isn't dangerous. I'm sure his directions are solid; he probably never even leaves that house— which made me wonder why he wanted the money. He's the only other soul in sight. It felt like we were embarking upon a scene out of the movie *Deliverance*; we just met the weird local— making him appear as though he were up to something as he sat there doing absolutely nothing.

"How far are we going?" my mom asks.

"From the map it's five miles" Andrew says, actually holding a map from the glove compartment this time.

"How far is that?" I ask.

"On the freeway, a few minutes. Here—I have no idea" my mother says as her voice trails off.

No idea. My poor mother didn't realize what she was getting into as our car entered the grove of shrouding trees leading towards the mountain. A caravan of strangers followed us—they were the other non-believers of the rockslide and we forced to join us on this excursion across the mountains.

There were no guard rails for the little dirt road that wrapped around the edges of the earth like twine on an egg. The ledges of the road revealed frightful cliff drops into a clouded, smoky abyss. My mother drove at a whopping ten miles an hour, as she was too scared to travel any faster because of the cliff's edge. I looked out the window and I couldn't even see the ground—just air. It was like we were floating across the mountains.

"Are we gonna fall?" I asked innocently, because it felt like it.

"I hope not. You buckled in?"

"Yes, why?"

"It's a long fall."

"So we shouldn't rock the car" says Andrew.

"Don't even think about it" our mother says with annoyance.

Made Genius

"I told you the freeway was closed" says Andrew.
"I know."
"Why didn't you believe it?"
"I didn't think it would be this bad."

Andrew and I got most of our devil-may-care approach to life from our mother, clearly, who ignores literal words of caution and takes off into the mountains with her children on the words of a mountain man with missing teeth who was smoking an ever-burning pipe and seemed legitimately crazy. My dad logicality had him flying in as close to the location of the family reunion as possible—we, my mother, brother, sister, Consuelo, and I, were all in the van leading an impromptu caravan...through the mountains...racing against the setting sun.

Spongey treetops decorated the vast sweeping, steep drops of the mountain range. My ears pressured up and popped a few times as we traversed the terrain. Consuelo prepared snacks that she distributed every forty-five minutes to keep us, the kids, occupied and from killing each other. Andrew had engaged himself in a book; I was lost in my own mind, dazed by the greenery. I wanted to live here, in this forest. I wanted to become part of the forest, the trees—leaves, the thick smoky fog would announce my presence; I'd wear a cloak, but it wouldn't be red like Red Riding Hood or other girls in the fables or fairytales, mine would be blue with a silver trim. I romanticized riding a horse through the mountains wearing my cloak—I imagined riding through the winds and turns at dusk, only to arrive at my village just before supper. Ah yes, I'd live a medieval life—

"Eat."

"What—I'm not hungry."

"Yes you are, eat."

I took a mini, crustless sandwich that Consuelo had pre-prepared for us to consume during the car ride; she had an entire cooler full of goodies.

By the time we exited that mystical forest and found the freeway again by some grace of god, it was dark. My mother hated driving in the dark and decided we needed to stay the night in a hotel. The first one we went to was all booked up—this is the 90's, so we couldn't exactly google a spot to go. The next four places also had no vacancy. Next place we went to had vacancy, but after my mother went to our room, we weren't there longer than a few minutes before she told us to grab our stuff.

"So why exactly are we not staying there" asks Andrew.

"Bad vibes" our mother says plainly.

"What do you mean?"

"That just wasn't a safe place, trust me. We are better off to keep looking."

Finally, a Holiday Inn had vacancy and our trek through the mountains ended. I wish I could say that was the strangest of things that ever happened going to a family reunion, but it wasn't; it was actually mild. My family has some kind of statistical-defying magnetism. Shit just happens.

JAMAICA

I was a frequent traveler and going to Jamaica was no different, it was once we got there that the issues started arising.

"When are we going to the hotel?"

"We aren't going to a hotel; we are staying in a house behind gates in a gated resort" my mother says to me.

"What, why?"

"This isn't a safe place Alexa, we are going to be staying at a fortress."

Our van arrived with a Jamaican man driving; he helped us with our luggage and soon we were on our way.

"Mom there's no seatbelts?"

"No, there aren't."

"Why?"

"They have different standards here."

"Standards? What about safe?"

"I told you, this isn't a safe place."

When we got to the house, I was shown by the maids to my room. However, I didn't stay there long because I saw a cat outside. I ran downstairs and out the door to follow it—we circled the house and then the cat rejoined its cat tribe; there were eight cats and four kittens. They were feral. Who cares! I love cats! My mother should've warned me that feral cats are like feral mice and feral rats—they carry diseases. Who cares! Animals! I had a few favorites by the end of the day. They let me touch them, hold them, and play with them. We were maybe fifty yards from the beach and the tall grass that separated the sand from golf grass is where the kitties liked to play.

During the evenings, there were bonfires at the main resort house and we went to them. There's a road to get to the main resort area, and halfway down the alley-like street is a random brick wall on the left hand side. The road is only passable on the right when going back towards the house. My mother doesn't like driving at night and we were in the golf cart—Somer, Andrew, and I. My mother was speeding along when I knew the wall was coming up, so I yelled "Wall!" and my mom swerved around it and broke and Somer went flying forward and slammed her head into the dash of the golf cart.

"She's bleeding!"

My mom looked stunned for a moment before turning to Andrew, "Take off your shirt."

"What, why? This is my favorite shirt."

"Just do it, I'll buy you a new one and something else you really want, okay?"

"Fine."

My mom applied pressure to the small gash above Somer's eye.

"Andrew I need to hold her, Alexa, keep pressure on her head."

"Okay, and then what?" Andrew says.

"We need Uncle Bill."

"What, why?" I ask.

"Because Alexa, He's a doctor and he might have a suture kit."

"Oh" I say.

"And we're in Jamaica. I don't want to go to a doctor here."

When we got back to the house, my mom left Somer, Andrew, and I in the care of the maid while she went down a few houses to where Uncle Bill was staying, and sure enough, he had his medical bag equipped with steri-strips and butterfly band-aids—good enough in a pinch. He came rushing over and fixed Somer right up. As he was walking away, I caught my toe on a tile and the sliced skin started to bleed profusely, so he came back with band-aids for me.

"Can you two stop getting injured for one day, just one day, that's all I ask."

When I went in the ocean the next day, the water stung my toe, so I opted not to go swimming anymore that trip. Instead, I played with the kitties I fancied. Big mistake. My mom didn't want me around the feral cats, so she took me to get my hair braided in cornrows and beaded. Afterward, she took me horseback riding—where the same lady that gave me cornrows was tending to the horses. Shocked and confused at first, I couldn't believe it was her. It must be a twin—we just saw her.
"Hello my dear, you've come to ride the horses?"
"Yes."
"Who would you like to ride?"

I walked up and down the stalls and found a liver chestnut gelding who was striking, even without much of a marking on his face. His name was Pretty Boy.

"Him, I want to ride him."

"Alright, we'll get Pretty Boy saddled up."

Horseback riding was fun; we walked and trotted around for a little bit—it was different than a trail ride. We were in an arena. I liked the feeling of being on a horse, their legs moving under me. I liked feeling their motion, the movement of their power beneath me. I felt stronger on a horse, natural. It was an emotion I've never felt and can't really describe.

On the way back to the house, we passed a golf cart full of Jamaican models doing some kind of photo shoot —I had seen them at the beach while my hair was being braided. When they saw me, they slowed down and smiled as they waved.

"We love your hair!"

"It's so cute!"

I had never really been liked by many of my peers at school up until this time, and these beautiful people thought I was cool. I wanted to be like them. Pretty, effortless, fun—I wanted to be beautiful.

When I got back to the house I started feeling sick, and then I got really sick—vomit. I started puking. Everything about my body felt weak. I felt awful, was I dying? It felt like I was dying. So hot, too hot, I'm all sweaty. My mom had Uncle Bill come over and he suspected some type of exotic flu. Exotic flu. Now where might I have gotten that?

"Is it contagious?"

"Doesn't seem that way."

"Could Somer or Andrew get sick?"

"Maybe, just keep her isolated and give her Tylenol for the fever."

Two days go by and I don't improve but now it's time to go home. I grab an oversized bag of KFC Barbeque chips even though I feel sick because I somehow bought them while I was still feeling well, and in my sick delirium, I didn't want to abandon the food. My mom was concerned by my behavior.

When we got to the airport, we waited on the tarmac for twenty minutes before we were informed that we had to go pick up the other passengers at another airport. I couldn't sit in my seat without feeling sick. I tried hard not to puke during the short flight, but then again, there was nothing in my stomach. A flight attendant comes up to me because I was leaning out into the aisle of the cabin.

"You need juice" says a Jamaican stewardess.

"What?"

"You're sick—you need the juice."

"My mom said I could only have water."

"You need the juice."

I turned around and looked down the aisle for my mother who made eye contact with me.

"What Alexa?"

"The Jamaican lady is telling me I need the Jamaican juice."

"You'll it throw up" she's says.

"I said thatand she said I need it."

"She needs the juice" says the Jamaican stewardess, whom was now leaning over our seats.

"Okay, fine. Have it—ask for a barf bag too."

The flight attendant disappeared down the aisle and came back with a lightly opaque orange-pink drink.

"Drink this."

"What is it?"

"Island juice."

"What kind?"

"Special Jamaican fruits."

Special Island Fruits she says—seems safe right? Maybe other people would turn down such an offer, but I was feeling too sick to care about what the hell that actually meant or what I was about to drink if it made me feel better. There is something mystical about the flight attendant, an earthy kind of vibration—I love good vibes and she had them, which I inherently trusted. I sipped on the juice which tasted like hints of pineapple, guava, papaya, passion fruit, orange juice, and something sweet I couldn't identify. I finished the drink and took a nap. When I woke up, we were landing. I did not throw-up. At first I was groggy, but then my energy escalated with my mood; I felt fantastic. I wouldn't have even known I felt so sick an hour earlier. It was like magic. What did she give me!? I'll never know, but when I'm sick, I mix all those drinks together into one and hope for the best.

6
FABULOUS FLORIDA

HORSES

There was a stable inside the gate-guarded neighborhood of our new home in Weston, Florida. We moved to Florida in August of 1999, but we had a beach house on the opposite coast of Weston and more north; it was in a place called Siesta Key, which is close to Sarasota. I begged my mom to take me to the stable in our new neighborhood, and finally she took me. I would spend all my spare time there. If I wasn't in school, I was at "the barn" as I called it. I wanted a horse in the worst way and eventually, I was surprised with the literal pony of my dreams who I named Pretty Boy, after a very special horse. Pretty Boy's show name was Fools' Gold because he's a light colored palomino with a white stripe and four white socks. He was very flashy and beautiful, "he looks like Barbie's pony" my mom joked. I rode at Windmill Stable and those girls became the first real friends that I could call friends. We all were horse-crazy and I loved every minute of it. Horses have a larger impact on me as I get a little bit older, so we'll revisit this momentarily.

~

READING

This is hard to explain; in the same way that my mind wandered in the smoky mountains as I gazed out of the window, my brain has the same knack for creating imagery as a process of understanding content. I'm seeing pictures, images, brief flashes of movement relating to the words I'm reading—it's all happening in my mind's eye simultaneously. At first that was overwhelming and impossible to decipher, but I started making the words a puzzle game, and eventually it began to make some sense.

~

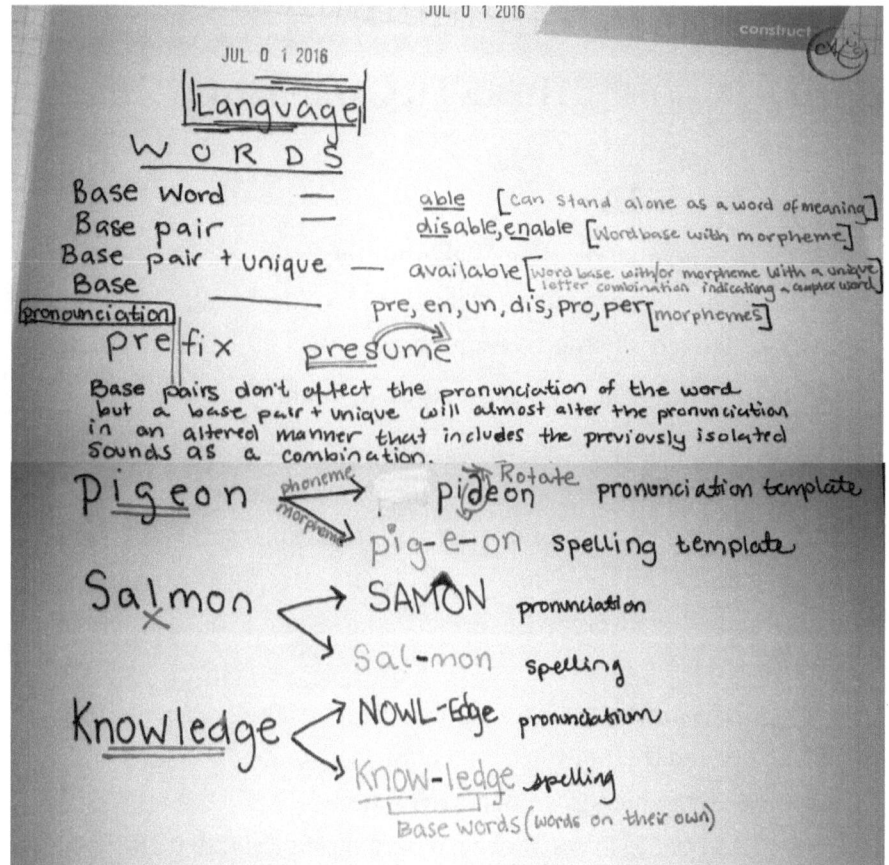

The diagram above is my best attempt to convey what I figured out as a child—it barely does my mental construction justice, but there's a web of interaction happening in my brain whenever I read something, and I know it can't be the same experience everyone else is having or they'd be living their life a little bit differently.

7
HOME TO CALIFORNIA

MICKEY

I remember meeting Mickey for the first time: I was looking for a equestrian coach after moving from Florida to California because my dad changed jobs, and was recruited to the CEO and President positions at $E_V{}^3$. Mickey is not a tall man, but his presence is at least double that of his physical size. He has this philosophical undertone to how he carries himself—book in hand, lanyard wrapped around his neck with his glasses hanging from it at rest on his chest; he loved wearing his old ivy cap from decades earlier. His posture wasn't rigid and straight like I would've expected from someone of his kind; the introverted kind, I mean.

He saunters as he walks—there is a certain synchronicity to his movement and rhythm—the connection from mind to body seems effortless, the same way a rider is to his horse.

As I got to know Mickey, it became apparent that his appearance matched what lay below the surface. His questions were always more pensive than probing.

I was only eleven years old when I met Mickey in the barn aisle of the Nellie Gail Equestrian Center in Laguna Hills. It was the first interview that I had ever been to, and it was terrifying in every way imaginable. My passion was about to be judged by a man that David Hume could've held a conversation with. I had only been living in California a few weeks; I didn't know anyone: new school, new barn, new people, new place; same pony. I was normally too shy and reserved to go out and do things for myself on my own when other people were involved, but here I was, checking out a stable where a girl from my new school rode. I overheard Christina talking about horses at school—turns out she's also my neighbor a few houses down the street; I asked her where she rode and she told me "With Mickey." *This might be it—I might finally fit in at school!*

When I arrived to the barn (which was actually a very nice, kept stable) on a Saturday morning, I found the main office where my meeting would be held; the office was between a bunch of stalls, because, *you know, horses.* Mickey stared at me with a kind of intent that no adult had ever given me before. The look questioned me, assessing my potential—for the first time, *I had potential to assess.*

"How serious are you?"

"Very."

He kept staring at me like I was supposed to do some kind of trick or say something so spectacular I'd catch him off-guard. I did not catch him off-guard unfortunately, but I could tell that I had piqued his interest with my ambiguous answer, on accident of course. I didn't know what I was doing but at the same time, I was always careful not to let people know what I'm really doing, or what I really want to achieve, just in case I can't or don't—not that I'm afraid to fail, but more that I don't want something to be such a struggle for once, and I liked surprising people. Life is more fun when people have no clue what you're about to do—or that's how I thought about it at least. And if I don't give one-hundred percent to my task, then I didn't feel so rejected by failure if and when I failed. I'm already my toughest critic, I didn't need anyone else telling me I couldn't do something I love doing because I'm not good at it.

"Have you shown before?"

"Yes, at Wellington in Florida."

Wellington is an Internationally ranked show circuit; while I participated in quite possibly the lowest level riding classes[9] available at the show, I still participated. It counts, I placed.[10]

"And what do you want to do?"

"The jumpers."

"Why?"

"There's more fences."

At current, I did the "hunters" which focuses on a rider's appearance and rider "etiquette" if you will. I hated it of course. In jumpers, I would be allowed to go fast and really *ride.* I was accepted into Mickey's riding program and my pony, named Mr. Pony (whom I called *Pony),* was hauled over to Laguna Hills from Lake Forest where he'd been living temporarily. Temporarily, because it was where my mom's friends Kris had horses, and we just moved to California so we had no clue where to go for training, or horse boarding.

---

[9] Class: A "class" in showjumping is a single event consisting of several competitors, sometimes hundreds, all whom of perform the same course of fences, with those going "clear" (no faults) to the next round. That second round is often referred to as the "jump-off" and it is scored under different "tables," depending on the class section. The table also informs the rider of how "time" will be converted to faults or time penalties, and when the jump-off will take place; either after every participant has gone in their first round as in *Table II, A,* or it follows immediately after the first round, as in *Table II, 2 B and C.* in *Table II, 2 B,* the rider waits for the buzzer before they are permitted to begin a jump-off, whereas in *Table II, 2 C,* the buzzer is a sign of elimination *from* the jump-off.

[10] Placed/Placing: refers to achieving a "place" in the order of 1-8th in a regular class, or 1-12th in a classic; classics award prize money for the first twelve in the order.

Made Genius

#

My first weekend at Mickey's was a little rough, if rough meant being flayed with an audience. Hayden Showjumping was having a "home show" that Saturday and Sunday, and I eagerly signed-up to participate. I couldn't wait to show everyone how cute my pony was and how great I was at riding. I had a very inflated ego—I knew a lot of what I *should do riding,* the problem was that I *didn't actually do those things while I rode*—unless I was showing and it counted, or because the judge at a show said so. It was one of those *keep your friends close, and your enemies closer* things—except that my "enemies" were actually the *competition*, and the *competition* were really my friends...so you could call me a hustler. I absorbed information but never acted on it until the moment was right. And at Mickey's, I had no idea what I was up against.

I was going to do a few jumper classes at the home show to see what it was like. While riding Mr. Pony in the top arena (there's three tiered arenas), Mickey noticed me having some struggles with Pony being "strong," (meaning the horse was pulling/hanging on the bit). Mickey came out of his personal office located in the corner of the club house and entered the arena over the side, which was only about twenty feet from his office window. He strode across the sand in a re-purposed, hostile manner; quick pace, visible momentum, and he was fixated on my pony. People parted away from me like Moses at the Red Sea to the water; their faces grimaced in anticipation of what was to come. I had absolutely no idea and wondered if I should now follow suit, but their faces told me that I couldn't. Instead of fleeing, I remained paralyzed by fear from Mickey's imminent and fast approaching confrontation; he yelled out to me.

"Are you just going to let that pony pull you around?"

"He's not pulling me, I–"

"–So you wanted him to rip off your little arms and not stop when he's supposed to–like a big bully?"

"No."

"So are you going to let him just pull you around?"

"No?"

"Was that a question?"

"No."

"Don't answer me with a question ever again. You give me an answer. And if you don't know, then say it."

"Okay."

"Are you going to let that pony pull you around?"

"No."

"Go jump that fence and halt."

I turned around and picked up the canter. Pony started to rush immediately, quicker and quicker to the fence, his stride lengthening to that of a large horse–he ran past the distance;[11] I have to either miss

---

[11] Distance: refers to the point at which a horse leaves the ground. *Deep* means the *distance* is incredibly close to the fence; whereas *short* means the strides *leading up to the fence* will create a closer distance. *Long* means the distance has a significant amount of space before the base of the fence; sometimes strides are left out of a line of fences to achieve this particular distance. There are benefits and risks of each distance according to the type of fence and its position within a course, and if it is part of a combination or not. A *medium* distance is not necessarily average, but provides minimal risk to most fences; however, achieving this distance consistently depends on the skill of a rider's "eye." And the "eye" of a rider refers to a rider's ability to judge the distance to fences accurately.

and chip,[12] or I let him take me to the long distance which will
invariably make halting impossible. I made the wrong decision and left
long, again. I tried not to; I wanted to wait for the deeper distance but
we couldn't. Pony got strong in the mouth and pulled me through the
corner. We spent the next forty-five minutes cantering, halting,
backing-up, and then repeating the process. Mickey's yelling got so
loud that people vacated the arena instead of just huddling in the
center. They stood on the outside of the arena watching the terror
unfold. The seating area started filling with spectators—other riders
and parents whose lessons got postponed by mine that was taking over
the night—they all watched my dignity get shredded by Mickey's verbal
jabs. Some people took notes; I didn't understand that at the time. It
made me feel like this whole spectacle was a cruel joke aimed at the
new girl, like some kind of initiation.

No one wanted to get in the way.

This is my first "Mickey-lesson" and it was horrifying from the
moment it began. How long the lesson would last remains to be
determined. I wanted to cry but I couldn't. I didn't want to show any
weakness because I was worried I would get yelled at for being "soft."
I didn't want to to anything that could compromise my position or give
Mickey ammo against me. I held it all in: excuses, my witty retorts,
complaints, pleas for mercy—I suppressed it. It wouldn't matter; if

---

[12] Chip: To add an extra half-stride or "step" at the base of a fence; often occurs
when the rider *misses* a distance, which means that the rider misjudged at what point
the horse is going to leave from the ground and consequently affected the horse's
take-off. A chip goes *past* the deep distance to a fence, and "chips" into the take-off
zone.

anything, it would work against me. I swallowed the knot in my throat, tightened my jaw, took a deep breath, and continued.

"Drop your stirrups."

The words I've been dreading to hear the whole lesson. Shit just got real. My arms were already aching, and now my legs were too, because I didn't have my stirrups to use as a crutch for balance. I dare not complain though. I just took another breath and endured this torment, hoping that I might be close to being done. It's now been two hours. I didn't even know it was possible to have a lesson go on for this long—apparently, Mickey is notorious for it; the notes—people take notes to avoid this. I started riding when it was still light out and now I'm surrounded by the darkness. The warm darkness felt like a blanket to hide beneath; I passed through pockets of cold air; I felt them every so often as I'd catch them passing through me. Suddenly, overhead arena lights came on and startled Pony; he took off bucking. *How nice for someone to illuminate the arena for me.* I leaned back and eventually Pony stopped. I did not complain still. I said nothing. Mickey had been silent until Pony stopped; I could almost feel the seething comment festering in the instance before he spoke—my anxiety spiked.

"You call that a halt? Pitiful. It takes two to pull."

I gave no response, no acknowledgement. I felt dazed, light-headed and dizzy, like I was in some other form of consciousness; I lost perception of my legs and arms. The constant pulling had become as dissociated as the repeating of a word over and over until you can't hear it anymore, it's just sound—this, this was just the vague sound of a feeling now, like a long-forgotten story that gets retold incorrectly until it no longer exists anymore. Is this delirium? It must be, but I cannot stop. Quitting is not allowed.

I tried to feel for limbs. My legs felt like Jell-o: jiggley, silly and losing tone. Like hitting your funny bone, and laughing so hard your sides hurt—but localized and focalized to one area of your body. I said nothing about this experience to Mickey. I had no idea why I was enduring this torture for something I thought I loved—*that's why I haven't quit yet.* I will not let go. I will not stop. I may be stubborn and doing this all wrong for the last two hours, but I wasn't going to stop until it was right. I couldn't; I love riding. It makes my soul sing—I can't be bad at this. It can't be like school, like reading. There has to be something I'm good at.

"Why are you doing the same thing over and over? You know what that is—it's insanity. You're insane. Do something different! WHAT ARE YOU DOING—Get his attention! He's running all over with you—anchor yourself. ARE YOU A SPACE CADET? DO YOU NOT LISTEN? You're all over! Use your legs—you have no legs, they're useless. You're kicking your pony—SQUEEZE. Squeeze him, use your muscles! MORE RIGHT LEG. Goo—NO! HANDS—WHERE ARE YOUR HANDS—HEELS, HEELS DOWN—HANDS, SHOULDERS BACK. YOU'RE LIKE A GRANDMA, A HAUNCHBACK, IT'S DISGUESTING. SHOULDERS BACK! RIGHT SHOULDER IS DROPPING, PUT IT BACK—SIT UP! LOOK UP! LOOK WHERE YOU ARE GOING AND FEEL. YOU'RE IN OUTER SPACE! YOU SPACE CADET, FEEL THE PONY—YOU WANT TO DO

THE JUMPERS? YOU CAN'T EVEN RIDE ON THE FLAT. FORGET JUMPING."

Forget jumping? This was my dream; I want to jump big fences, and I needed to be better. Every criticism he attacked, I adjusted myself instantly so it no longer existed. He repeated, I repeated. Closing in on three hours, he finally let me have a break, but it wasn't the one I wanted. I wanted to keep going. I didn't need to feel my limbs, *they were useless anyway.* I needed to be good. Mickey could make me good. I could hear it in the way he was so determined to make me *get it*—get this experience in his mind that he wanted to transfer to me, but I didn't get it; I tried to and I was close, just not close enough.

"THAT'S IT—YOU'RE DONE. BE DONE. I can't take this anymore. YOU'RE NOT GETTING IT. IF YOU WANT TO RIDE HERE, YOU NEED TO TOUGHEN UP. If you want me to teach you, you need to be willing to learn."

There were at least fifty people watching that entire episode. Humiliated. That's how I felt—how could that man do that to me, I'm young, just a kid and I wanted to learn. I did want to learn, or thought I did. Didn't I try this time? I'm new to him, he's new to me; I wanted to make a good impression. No, I wanted to make a great impression, for once. Maybe I didn't try—I thought I tried; how do I know if I tried hard as I could have? *Should I go back into the ring? Or should I be done—did I try—do I protest?*

I walked back to my stall feeling rather defeated. I took off Pony's tack and put him away. I groomed him superficially because I was going to come early in the morning and bathe him before the showmanship class. However, as I walked away from Pony's stall, everything I just went through started cascading its effect into this flashback of a traumatic experience.

When I got in my mom's car, it was the first safe place I had been all day—I broke down crying. I was so upset I couldn't even explain what just happened. I hated everything about Mickey—I didn't really, I just thought that I did at that moment because I had never been cut down by an adult before, not like that. It's one thing when your parents yell at you, it's completely different when your coach comes at you.

My peers had done it all my life, *bullying I mean,* but I never had an adult do what Mickey did. Usually in sports, it was all *encouragement* and *A's for effort.* Mickey liked effort, but he *also* liked results more. If I wasn't getting results, then the effort was being misapplied. My mother had no sympathy for me—partly because she couldn't understand a goddamn word I said crying as hysterically as I was, and also because she and I made an agreement years earlier, when we lived in Florida. My friend, Ali Marino (Dan Marino of the Miami Dolphin's daughter), would have meltdowns about showing, riding, and her horses. My mom took one look at that and then told me that if I ever looked like she did, we'd be done. No more horses.

"What have I told you about crying because of riding?"

"Not to do it."

"Right. Why is that?"

"Because it should be fun. If I'm crying, then I'm stressing myself out and not having fun."

"Correct. You don't have to do the show tomorrow. I'm going out to dinner with your father. No crying. Do what you want. So why are you crying?"

"I had a long day."

My parents were somewhat alienating when it came to my emotional difficulties, but they had good intentions behind it. They wanted me to be "emotionally strong," not someone who gets coddled when the challenges are difficult or whines about criticism. They raised me to be as honest with myself about my talent and ability, and to see myself through the eyes of my best coach and worst critic. Hard work is hard work. You reap exactly what you sow.

❦

My mom came home from dinner later that night and I was in one of the downstairs bathrooms polishing my tall boots—the tack had been cleaned already. My saddle and bridle looked polished and perfect laying across a makeshift saddle stand of chairs.

"Oh, I see you're doing the show tomorrow?"

"Yes."

"What changed your mind?"

"I want to be a great rider."

"I knew you'd make up your mind."

The next morning, I did showmanship and won the class. I did the flat class right after it and came in second out of fifteen. My competition was Mickey's riders in his current training program, on both his and their own horses.

When the jumping started, it was hunters first, so I had to wait for the jumpers later in the morning. Hunters is about etiquette, tradition, and appearances; it demands very little in the realm of how well someone rides. It's all about how you look, not what you can do. I made a decision about what I planned to do. I didn't ride to win; I rode to prove a point. *I wanted to win*, but winning would cost me more than losing in this instance, for later. I had to show Mickey that I could ride. I half-halted Pony on the way to each fence so he wouldn't pull me; I resisted every long distance that I could. Pony got strong and took a long distance to one fence by the gate, so I circled and took the four faults for it because I knew if I didn't, Pony would snowball out of control. I didn't get a ribbon in that class, but in the next jumper class I got fourth and I still rode well—not for the long distance either, and I didn't let Pony pull me. Afterward, Mickey came up to me:

"I heard you took it rough yesterday. I want to let you know that I'm trying to get under your skin to motivate you—don't take anything I say personally. You did good today. What you did yesterday made today easier. It's going to get better."

He walked away.

Mickey was notorious for ripping people apart during lessons in a constructive-criticism sort of way, and not a lot of people could withstand his technique because most were pretty soft with deep pockets, but he did create incredible riders in those that stayed. They won all the time, even on different and unfamiliar horses in places they had never been before. Mickey taught a well-rounded equestrian curriculum; it wasn't enough to ride your own horse well, you had to be able to ride *any* horse well. And on those rare days where it rained in Southern California, we would do what is called an "in-house" lesson, where we watched riding videos frame-by-frame and picked apart the rider and horse; it reminded me of my first lesson with Mickey. Those sessions lasted well over an hour—sometimes they were as long as four hours and on Saturday, that easily turned into lunch.

Mickey liked people to switch horses if they were having a hard time with their own, sometimes everyone in the lesson played musical horses. He also offered "extra" horses, or horses that needed to be exercised, and he encouraged everyone to leave a note on the board if they had time to ride "extras" one day; you could ride more than one extra too. I had six horses a few times. Every single one I rode, I practiced everything that I was learning in my lessons: soft, supple; round, on-the-bit and moving through[13].

When everyone else was letting their horses stand and get cold during lessons, I was walking–constantly working so I'd be ready when it was my turn. I didn't work as hard as I did just to get sloppy when we became fatigued. The mind is an incredible force. Sports have that saying that its "ninety percent mental and ten percent physical ability," and I agree with that whole-heartedly.

---

[13] Moving through: refers to a horse's movement from the haunch "through" the forehand and into the bit which creates "impulsion" or pliable momentum. When a horse is "on the bit," the rider has created a straight line from the horse's pole to the ground, which causes the horse's neck to curve/arch in response to the desired movement.

I rode this horse named Florian one day, and he was a little bit prissy when it came to anything unfamiliar, complicated, or physically requiring. Mickey thought it would be "interesting" if I rode Florian in my lesson one day. At first, I was excited to have two lessons: one on my horse, one on Florian; that is, until I learned why nobody liked to ride him for a certain reason; he is a big baby. Going to the black-panel fence, Florian started to suck back—I legged him forward but he stuck the take-off because the black panels were the equivalent of jumping over a black hole, at least in Florian's mind; I kicked him forward. I was imagining all the scrutiny I'd receive from Mickey if he stopped, I'd rather get yelled at for kicking instead of squeezing. *Results>tradition.* Florian jumped straight up and flung his head into the air, consequently popping me in the nose and mouth with his big head. I was bleeding from the nose and mouth. No matter, *I was fine.*

"Do you need to take a break?"

"No."

"Are you sure? You can take a break if you need to."

"I said I'm fine!"

I never asked for break. The only breaks that I took was one that were forced upon me. I had this compulsion to keep trying to do something until I finally did it correctly. Academically, that's great. Work ethic—even better, but mentally, *that's how people go insane.* So while sometimes it seemed like a good thing, other times it could be the beginning of a downward vortex. Lane, Mickey's protégé, started training me when I began jumping bigger and becoming more and more stubborn. Lane is only five years older than me and took no shit from anyone—and he could call me on my BS. Not that I necessarily had BS with Mickey, but Lane got inside my head to how I thought; he knew my instincts.

My friends joked that riding with me was a gamble because I'd either consume all the negative criticism, or I'd set Mickey off, and then no one was safe from ridicule. On the other hand, Lane was diplomatic in lessons, but I earned the place of his guinea pig for the "experimental" exercises he would build. If we weren't sure an exercise would fly, I'd get to try it first. Lane would begin the lesson, and then Mickey would finish, or we'd get divided, sometimes, Mickey would pick on just one person and they'd get singled out from the lesson; sometimes Lane was the trainer with one person to coach, and then Mickey was the one with a group. It changed frequently and was unpredictable. It largely depended on Mickey's mood compared to everyone's effort and ability that day. The more I wanted just one trainer and for things to be expected, the more their style seemed to evolve and change. It was probably coincidence.

~

Mickey found my mare Natana in Del Mar; Lane was given a "sale" mount and rode her for The Beverley Hills Equestrian Center, but when Lane got on, he had a different revelation; "Mick, I think this one would be good for Alexa to try." So I did, but one caveat; I'm the pickiest horse-trier. Some people are really picky eaters, I'm really picky about the horse I ride—in competition.

I'll ride anything for "funzies," but my competition horse has high standards to be met. So when I went to try the mare, Mickey wouldn't let me decide I didn't like her by not letting me get the chance. He was literally going to rush me into everything like throwing a kid into a pool and shouting "swim or tread water!"

"You're going to get three warm-up fences and then you're going in."

"Why only three?"

"Because, you'll figure it out better in the ring."

"What?"

"No complaining about anything the horse does strange—it has a funny mouth."

"Great."

I pull back, the mare roots[14] on the bit and I can't steer for a moment. *Fantastic.* I don't know this mare is a mare at the time I was riding her, I think she's a gelding. In hindsight, her being a chestnut mare explains it all. That's their stereotype—being crazy and such, the same way that gingers don't have souls. I get in the ring and after fence five, there's a rollback by the entry gate to a vertical near the stands; when I went to turn, the horse did not turn.

"It's okay, you can circle." I hear shouted from the sidelines; Mickey, Lane, my best friend Paige, and my father are all standing there.

*No. I will **not** circle. I will not take the easy way out.* So, I sat deep and really used my outside leg and did not release the inside rein

---

[14] Roots: Refers to a horse lunging its forehand weight on the bit, hangs, bites the bit, or otherwise prevents the proper utilization of the bit.

through the turn until I felt the horse yield; it was a battle of wills. We *barely* made it to the fence without missing it. We ended up placing third in that class. I was rather pleased that we placed. She was a "three-foot jumper," meaning that is the height she can comfortably complete a course at. A more experienced rider could take her higher, but it would take the correct ride to each fence, and it would be tough for her athletically. I didn't believe any of that crap for a second.

Outfitted in a "Pessoa," a lunging rig designed by Olympian Rodrigo Pessoa meant to engage the horse's hindquarters, my task of building muscle began. In the Pessoa, and me on foot, Natana and I went jogging on the trails at least once a week up and down the hills to build muscle. I told my friends, "if she has to do it, then so do I." One day a week, usually Fridays, I worked on teaching her how to turn from the ground. I taught her cues and new ways to understand the jumps.

However, that mare taught me how to ride too, and together, we won and accomplished more than anyone expected of us. We even beat her old owners and won the class against the horse that replaced her.

"How'd you get her to jump like that?"

"Training."

"No really—did you pole her?"

"No really, we worked hard on the flat. We basically retrained her."

"She looked great."

Mickey smiled as he told me the interaction between him and the other trainer.

"You can't buy your way out of hard work."

I looked at him confused for a moment.

"A lot of these parents, they don't want to hear that their kids aren't good enough—or that they need to work. They need to put blood, sweat, and tears into what they're doing to get good, and most parents, most parents don't want their kids to struggle. They don't want them to learn how to be strong and they'll never be good riders. Their parents will just keep buying nicer and nicer horses until they ruin them or run out of money."

Not even the best trained horse can beat a well-trained rider. I took that mare Natana into the 1.30 division and won. I got her for the 1.10's. Lane was right—Natana taught me more about riding than any human ever could alone, but with Mickey and Lane, Natana and I

Alexa on Natana   *October 15, 2006*

became champions. We won everything and were fearless in the show ring. We even beat Lane in a high jump at a home show. I still remember that fence, the way it felt; Natana's powerful stride charging towards the fence to the most perfect distance—she was a force of nature that I'd been blessed to ride. Her name meant "gift" in Hebrew—I looked it up. And a gift she was. Mickey came up to me after, much like he'd done in the past and spoke to me with a sense of pride I hadn't heard before.

> "Knowing you, and knowing your horse—I never would've believed that you two were capable of that—especially not her with her with your inexperience jumping big fences—that was incredible. You're destined for great things A-Lex!"

He poked me in the nose with his finger like you push an arcade start button, and then he turned to walk away, placing his hand on my shoulder as he passed by. That was my graduation from pony-rider to true equestrian. My mentor was finally proud, fulfilled—after all of the tears, the sweat, the blood, he was right; you cannot buy your way out of hard work, or that feeling when it all comes together. It was beautiful—one of the greatest moments of my entire life. It wasn't just the fence, it was Mickey; without him, the fence would've been a really large jump, not an obstacle I could overcome. But because of Mickey, it was the first limit I learned to break; it set me free, he set me free. He was the beginning of my achievements.

∾

Years later, when my dad sold Natana to Mickey because "daddy suddenly decided not to support my riding anymore," Mickey let me decide what he should to do with her. He owned her, and he was letting me decide her fate. Of course I wanted to keep Natana, but I knew I couldn't. I was crying in Natana's stall after hearing the news because I didn't want to lose her. My dad literally showed up at my school, in the parking lot by my car during break, and just nonchalantly said, "hey, sold your horse." And then he left. Just left. She was my best friend. So no way in hell was I about to go back to class after that—I left. I went straight to the barn hoping she was still there. That's when Mickey confronted me.

"Do you want me to keep her in the barn, or find her a good home somewhere else? Would it be harder for you to see her everyday, or would you like being able to check-up on her?"

Mickey also let me ride Natana in the IEL horse shows for my school during senior year, even though she wasn't mine anymore. He let me ride her a few times after that, even after someone was already leasing her. Mickey told me that I always have horses to ride at his barn if only I ask. I used to be scared of him, but Mickey has become one of

 my most treasured friends and remains a treasured mentor of mine. He changed my life by showing me what real excellence looks like and can do; he conditioned me to persevere past the toughest obstacles, and I've transcended that ability from the equestrian world into that of writing. There's is no doubt in my mind that Mickey is the reason that I am a prolific writer, and I'm honored that his character was able to leave its mark on mine.

DOWN IN VISTA

I sat cross-legged on the couch in my therapist's office; we were discussing the most recent string of events that has prompted a restrictive parameter for my gallivanting.

"Do you know why you're here?"

"Because I forgot to charge my phone."

Why did saying that make me want to laugh? With eager patience, my therapists asked me to recount the catalyst to my current circumstances:

My friend, Victoria Cooper, left Mickey's and moved her horse back to her house in Vista, California. I was a few years younger but nevertheless, she invited me over. Apparently she had a house on several acres that included a stable, riding arena, and a lake with its own island. Victoria is the grand daughter of the same Mr. Cooper who designed the first mini cooper car in the UK. Her dad told me about a rally race story that involved them totaling a cow, and a car, and how it led him to redesign how the car handled—it gave them the mini.

I was seventeen at the time and feeling overly confident in my notoriously poor navigation skills; I failed to print the instructions on how to get to Victoria's house from mine. I had my phone and because of traffic, and my excessive use of it at full brightness; the battery depleted and entered the critical and unpredictable 10% battery life zone. I say "unpredictable" because during this time, a phone could shutoff anywhere from

1-10% with the same prevalence. I tried to memorize the instructions, repeating the address over in my head in case I had to stop and ask someone how to get there. I should've asked someone how to get there after my battery died, but I didn't–overconfident-Alexa can memorize anything, she knows the way! I did not know the way, I mean, I sort of did but I swear to god it was just like a series of ridiculous events that kept happening despite my best efforts to stop the cascade unfolding.

I turned down highway 85...or was it 59? There was a five in there...It was something like that, the numbers weren't really important because the road went by another name of a K.I.A. police officer, who's name I also forgot–I knew where I was going and that's the important thing, or so I thought.

I turned down the road and then turned onto the street where Victoria supposedly lived. Calling it a "street" is an understatement–narrow, rural highway is far more accurate. I drove up and down this highway for forty-five minutes looking for the number "25530" and that's when I began to wonder whether it was "23350" because I saw the entrance to that lot. Fives were really messing me up that day. Now it was well-past lunch time, so I decided to go to the alternate address instead of the one I memorized. First, I drove up a hill behind avocado groves. "This is clearly incorrect," I thought to myself. Driving my Mitsubishi eclipse, which is a wannabe sports car, I proceeded down a dirt road. After about ten minutes I decided that this was the wrong direction, I even said to myself, "this cannot be right." In my attempt to back out, I backed into a ditch.

"That's unfortunate" I think to myself. My excellent teenage logic thought backing my car farther into the ditch might allow me to drive it out; that was incorrect reasoning. My car tilted upright at a sixty-degree angle, resting on its back bumper. Fantastic. Now it's really stuck. I turn off the engine, take my purse and dead phone, and begin to proceed back down the dirt road when all of a sudden, I heard what I thought were dirt bikes in the distance.

How many horror movies, action movies, and thrillers have I seen? I know this can't possibly end well knowing there's drug cartels in the area.

I look to my left and there fifteen feet to a ditch that is at the base of an incredibly steep hill that has trees growing out of it horizontally. It's a sideways forest? Paranoid, precautious—I sprint and leap up as I grab hold of the exposed roots or trunks of some little trees and hoist myself up into them. I climbed up into the trees a few more feet so that I was still hidden, but I didn't want to be so far up that I couldn't see what passed by. Two men, both on ATV's with Ak-47's strapped across their backs, flew by.

"This is how I die. I am going to die out here because I forgot to charge my fucking phone and I can't navigate." I was a girl scout. They left me in the woods and I made it back—why can't I just go have lunch with my friend at her house—why can't I have nice things? "No, I do not accept that outcome." I'm going to figure a way out of this...

I look again to my left and maybe twenty feet from my position is a barbed wire fence—but the fence intersects the hill and I am high enough in the trees that I could literally, just hop over the barbed wire unscathed.

I'm going to do it. You can do it. I'm doing this. Deep breath.

Purse first, then myself. I walked no more than a few steps before I heard grinding sounds—metal. Metal grinding into something dense. The narrow aisle-like walkway that I jumped into split to the left and right, and the grinding sounds as if it's coming from the lower right side; the pathway sloped downward out of sight. I stayed to the left and encountered several caged animals—abused animals, from their scars and reactions towards a person—me. I happen to be an animal lover and I went to take a picture with my phone, which was dead of course—*this is why you're in this mess; your phone is dead. You can't even take a picture.*

There was a camel, llama, miniature donkey, a pony, two goats, and some chickens. I unlatched their cages as I walked by—if they got out then that was their own fault, I merely provided an opportunity. *I hope they break free.* I see the right side of the path merge back with mine up ahead, and I can see that it splits again about one hundred feet ahead of me. On the right hand side of the right-sided path is the barbed wire fence, hidden behind trees in giant wooden pots shaped like squares. There's a smaller hut-looking-shack at the end of a row of trees a hundred feet away on that right-sided path. I resolve to walk towards the barbed wire fence. There's some wooden, square-shape pallets leaning upright against the hut-shed thing. After pondering it for a moment, I decided that I could use one of the wooden pallets and lay it across the potted trees and the top of the barbed wire fence and crawl across to freedom.

As I approach the trees to execute my plan, a German Shepard charges towards me from out of nowhere, barking voraciously.

Shit. Shit. Shit. *I am so dead right now.* He's going to blow my cover with his barking and then he's going to maul me to death. I'm going to die getting mauled by a dog—no, no! That's a terrible way to die. No. I can get out of this. I have to.

I look around and I see a 2X4 lying on the ground—I lunge for it and hold it like a bat.

"I don't want to do this dog, but if it's me or you—I'm choosing me, sorry."

The dog skidded to a stop but continued to bark, so I sprinted to the potted trees. I had to hide and hope they didn't go looking for what set the dog off. As I positioned myself behind a potted tree, one guy came out of the shed to reprimand the dog. When he went back in, I crept over and peeked in the window as I grabbed a wood pallet. Bricks of white were stacked like small sandbags on the table; it was coke—they were cutting cocaine. Drugs.

I *so* need to get the hell out of here. I am going to get killed by a drug cartel. No, I need to get to a public place, I need to be out in the open—I have to get out of here.

Hastily, I placed the wooden pallet over the potted tree and barbed wire, but as I started to crawl across, the dog began barking and adrenaline shot down my spine like lightning. I slipped, tore my Rock & Republic jeans, but rolled the landing and managed not to cut myself—unscathed still. I grabbed my purse, the 2x4, and ran as fast as my legs and lungs would take me to the main road.

I reached the main road and across the street was a call box, almost like I was being taunted by the universe because it was too easy. What other choice did I have? The only call I could place was to the operator, who made me want to smack my head into a wall.

"Hi, my car is in a ditch; I need a tow truck for my 2007 Mitsubishi Eclipse. It's black."

"Okay you need a tow truck. Where are you?"

"I don't know, I'm calling from a landline—don't you know where I am?"

"Oh yes Ma'am, I can see where you are calling from now. Thank you. Make and model of the car?"

"Mitsubishi, Eclipse."

"I got a Mitsubishi. What was the model ma'am?"

"Eclipse."

"Right. And you wanted a tow truck?"

"Yes. Because my car is in the ditch."

"Are you with the car ma'am?"

"No, I'm on the phone with you—my car is in a ditch."

"Okay ma'am, I'm going to need you to stand out by the road where you'll be visible to the driver coming to assist you."

No way in hell was I about to sit and wait outside the entrance to my near-death-experience. I observed the traffic for a few minutes and started walking in the direction that I saw the most cars coming from. And after about thirty minutes, I saw the tow truck driver so I flagged him down. The problem with what happens next is that the driver was being tailgated by a Range Rover, and the tow truck wasn't exactly all the way on the shoulder. I instinctively took a step back after seeing the imminent outcome, there was almost no time to react—a piece of the Range Rover's front bumper goes flying past me and misses me by inches. *Is someone trying kill me, am I supposed to die today or something?* No. I refuse. Nope. You can't have me.

I went over to the driver of the tow truck.

"Hey man, you've probably got to deal with this um—incident-accident ordeal, so I'm going to leave you my mother's number. My phone is dead so you can't call me. Coordinate with my mother about getting my car out of the ditch, I'll be back in an hour—I think my friends house is up the street."

"Okay, very good."

It turns out that the tow truck drive didn't really speak English so my mom got a message that was something along the lines of: Your daughter drove her car into a ditch, was involved as a pedestrian in a two car traffic accident, and that I fled the scene.

I fled the scene.

Two police helicopters were authorized to search the area I was believed to be in. My mother called every single person that she knew that I knew, and eventually, she figured out from Lane that I was supposed to be going to have lunch with

Victoria down in Vista. How Lane came about that information is also beyond me. But when my mother called Mrs. Cooper, she found out that I never arrived, which of course sent my mother into a panic. At the time, I had no idea there was a Search & Rescue crew searching for me from the air. They couldn't find my car either which only fueled anticipation over finding me. How do I get myself into these situations, right?

Maybe this is the point in which one would decide to flag someone down and ask for a ride, or a phone charger perhaps— maybe an actual phone? (The year is 2008) I wanted to cross the highway, so I made sure there weren't cars coming first, but as I sprinted across the road, my phone fell out of my pocket— without thinking I lunged back for it only to find myself standing on the narrow strip of paint dividing the road, with a burst of cars flying past me on either side. Idiot. *You're going to die now for sure—you're going to get hit by a car for not looking before you stepped back into the road, and now you're stuck in the middle.* I closed my eyes, I took a deep breath. I couldn't move for the next five seconds at least and it felt like minutes; if I looked at what I was trying not to accidentally lean into—I was going to accidentally lean into it—it being the line of cars passing. I opened my eyes to a window of opportunity—a break in traffic to the other side of the road, I took it. *That was very dumb and I'm very lucky.*

I walk away from the road, over a grass mound and onto an unobstructed street with a few houses on either side. Most of them looked weathered and unkempt, but there was a man watering his lawn at the house nearest to me. How bad could this go? I had forgotten how I might be perceived because I was very much inside my own head. I was limping from running and walking so much after having foot surgery earlier that week, and now there was a 2x4 slung over my shoulder. As I approached, the guy started to back away—he went all the way into his house and locked the door. Then his dog came running out at me—oh hell no. not again; and here I was the one afraid to even walk up to him. Just as I was about to turn and run he called off the dog, which stood motionless a few feet from me and off the to the side of the house; I approached with a significant amount of caution. Then I knocked on his door which had grid of windows on the top half, so he could see me and I could see him, very easily. He talked at me through the glass.

"What do you want?"

"My phone died—It's an apple iPhone, and I drove my car into a ditch. I was wondering if you might have a phone charger I could use for a few minutes to charge my phone up and make a call?"

"I only have an iPod charger."

"Oh, that won't work. Thanks anyway."

"Goodbye."

He turned around and walked away, so I did the same. The dog followed me to the edge of the property line. I continued down the road as I heard the chopping of air above Helicopters? Must be here for the car accident with the tow truck. I had no idea those choppers were out and about looking for me. After failing to find me at this point, my mother called her friend at the police station who was a motorcycle cop, and he got in touch with his buddies at CHP and they got *another* helicopter in the air.

Meanwhile, I was walking down the shoulder of the rural highway with a 2x4 slung over my shoulder completely unaware of any rescue efforts. Not many people can say that they've walked completely lost down a California desert highway in the thick of the day with a 2x4 over their shoulder, but I can. It was hot; I was tired and thirsty. I just wanted to be done and go home. But I couldn't. I didn't care about going to lunch with Victoria anymore. Eventually, the seemingly endless road curved into a blind turn; I came to a gated entrance off the side of the road. Behind the gate was a street that rounded a corner up a hill out of sight. I had driven past the golf course that followed at least six times looking for Victoria's house. Now that I've walked all the way here, I know just how far I've actually walked, which was somewhere between 6 miles. I walked up to the keypad and noticed there was an operator button. Another operator. Fantastic. I pressed the button and stared into the camera near the keypad.

"Hello?" A gentle, feminine voice came out of the keypad.

"Hi, hello—I was wondering if you could do me an odd favor?"

"What would that be?"

"Could you maybe google my friends address? I'm lost—I drove my car into a ditch, the tow truck driver got in a car accident trying to help me, my phone is dead, I had toe surgery the other day and I have been walking for the past six hours. I just want to go home."

"Hold on, I'm sending someone to get you."

"To get me?"

There was no response after that.

Sending someone to get me? A "someone" certainly arrived; he came in a golf cart. Together we went up the hill out of sight, only to emerge from the miniature forest of trees at some kind of dreamy oasis—am I on drugs, what is happening? Little cabana houses lined the sides of the street and then we crossed over a lake towards a bigger building. Where was I? Then I saw the golf course off in the distance and people carting themselves around. What the hell?

"What is this place?"

"It is a men's day spa retreat."

"You certainly are hidden."

"Our clientele tends to be high-profile and want to be discrete."

He stopped beneath a porta cache and I was escorted into the operator's office. She was a nice woman in her thirties. Immediately, she offered me apricot water and a seat. I took both. She couldn't let me use the phone because I was technically not supposed to be there, and she was on camera, but she offered me an interesting compromise. I was reluctant to take the offer at first given how my day unfolded, but I was desperate to go home, so I just agreed perhaps a little too readily to the terms. I waited ten minutes and then when one of her employees was leaving for the day, she took me with her to search for my friend's house, one last time. Because I was sure this time I would find it. I didn't know my mom was worried, so I didn't think to try calling her either.

I left with the nice younger woman who ran the day spa store. For ten minutes we drove around before I had a feeling to drive down an unmarked street. Then I saw the numbers, the arena—the lake with its island. I found Victoria's house! This was it, why the hell was it down an unmarked street—did that escape Victoria's mind when we were talking about how to get here? I got out and ran to the door. Mrs. Cooper answered and invited me in.

"People are looking for you."

"What—Why?"

"Apparently you're missing."

"Funny, I thought I was lost."

"This isn't the time for jokes—call your mother and tell her you're okay."

I reluctantly waited for my phone to charge and then once I had enough battery life, I dialed my mom's number. At first she didn't answer so I had to call her back. That time she answered.

"Where the hell are you?"

"Victoria's house."

"What happened to you earlier?"

"Oh. I got lost."

"You got lost."

"Yeah, and my phone died" I say without any sense of accountability.

"Why didn't you find a phone."

"I tried. There were some strange situations."

"I'm sure."

"No really, I swear."

"Okay, you're staying the night there. I don't want you driving back, in the dark after this fiasco. And from now on keep your phone charged, and you're no longer allowed to leave Orange County without permission before and a charged phone. And a means of charging it if it dies."

"Okay, fine."

"And go get your car."

"Okay. I will."

"Ugh, I will see you tomorrow."

"Okay, sorry for stressing you out."

"I'll see you tomorrow."

Just then, Mr. Cooper walks in the door and sees me next to his wife.

"See, I told you she'd resurface."

"Yes she did, but without a car."

"Where's your car?"

"In a ditch."

"Of course it is. Well let's go get it."

I sat in the passenger side of an old truck and led the way to my car. We drove down Victoria's unmarked street onto the highway and three miles down the road. We turned into the open lot and drove all the way back to my car. We waited for the tow truck driver, whom helped liberate my poor coupe. But as my car made its way to solid ground it ran out of gas. Mr. Cooper frowned at me. It's not like I planned to do laps on the rural highway until my tank was almost empty, only to drive it into a ditch...

After staying the night, I found out that Victoria made other plans with her boyfriend in the morning, and since I disappeared, she thought I wasn't coming. We only saw each other briefly in the morning before she left. But since I was awake so early, Mr. Cooper showed me where Dillon, Victoria's horse, was. I got him ready to ride. And after riding for an hour, that's when I returned home to receive the wrath of my mother, which interestingly was more annoyed than angry. *If only my phone were charged.* I think that a lot. Then I realize that little detail is the reason these ridiculous shenanigans ensued, that, and maybe my radar for danger operates on a different frequency.

After telling the entire story to my therapist, he just sat there smiling at me for a while.

"What?"

"Don't you think it's comical?"

"What's comical?"

"You don't find it comical that the part they are angry about is your irresponsibility with your cell phone—not the ridiculous situations that you got yourself into?"

"Hey, I didn't get myself into anything. I was just trying to have lunch with my friend and then things happened like they always do."

"I know."

GULL LAKE

In 2002, the Corbett Family reunions found a recurrent location at Gull Lake in Minnesota. We drove three hours after taking a three-hour flight just to get there. Minnesota has 10,000 lakes, so of course we have to drive three hours to get to one in specific. The little town of Nisswa and Brainard were close by and were good tourist locations for shopping and other things to do. The lake had canoes and a small powerboat for us to use. Andrew and I were notorious for getting into something potentially dangerous and certainly forbidden.

To operate a boat or jetski you needed a license, no matter for Andrew—he'll just figure it out without one. With our cousin Ryan along for the ride, we set off across the lake as fast as the motor would take us.

"Sit in the bow."

"The Front?"

"It's scary up there, no."

"I can't see; I need you to weigh it down."

Maybe someone would've taken offense to that, like are you calling me fat? But instead, I did as I was instructed and Ryan took control of the engine, and turned it so hard and fast that the boat tipped all the way onto its side; it flopped right-side-up once it came through the turn. It was absolutely terrifying and I demanded to be brought back to shore. We were in the middle of the lake—I saw *Lake Placid*, no one needs to tell me twice not to be stupid in a creepy lake. I did not want to be in, around, or near a sinking boat.

❦

Gull Lake is where I first got drunk and Andrew caught me.

"You idiot. Go drink some water" he says.

"I'm not thirsty" I said confidently as I walked right into a wall.

"Yeah, I'm sure you're fine."

Andrew could be a real smart ass sometimes, but most times, it was warranted.

8
Past Portraits

By now, you probably have a pretty good understanding of who I was as a child; I'm sure even in childhood there were profound instances of definitive transformation.

And in regard to my initial narrative in *Wisdom 23* and in *24: Wiser Fools,* certain aspects of the story—my story, still hadn't been fully actualized, at least in regard to my experience, which was contrasted by the reality my parents *thought* they were projecting onto me

To fully understand why I became *so* determined to persevere despite the constant adversity can be found in the result of the testing I mentioned having at the start of this book.

When I was seven years old, my "educators" gave up on me because I was too difficult to teach and just "didn't learn." I was literally illiterate.

Eligibility Determination

Existence of disability: ■ Yes ❑ No

Student is making effective progress in regular education: ❑ Yes ■ No

Eligible for special education services: ■ Yes ❑ No

(image excerpt from IEP evaluation by the Commonwealth of Massachusetts, 1998)

Fearing for my future success, my parents had me evaluated by three different professionals multiple times to determine the problem with my learning—which kept revealing some kind of issue: dyslexia. My parents agreed to intervention but then also never told me about it or "why" I was doing "special classes," or what was "wrong" with my learning.

As mentioned previously. Dr. Kuncaitis found indications of a specific learning disability, dyslexia. Analysis of Alexa's performance on this evaluation also indicates manifestations of dyslexia, which may be complicated by additional language-based learning disabilities. That

(from an evaluation by a third party, 1998)

I had special programs meant to aid me that failed; I was still incredibly illiterate despite massive intervention, which in my parents' opinion, was negligent on part of the school—as they voiced concern long before my issue went critical and held me back a grade.

The evaluator noted that I had successfully identified words "by what they looked like" rather than using letters as cues to sounding it out. I legitimately had no clue how to read.

Made Genius

Then finally, at ten years old I had taught myself.

People who know me are probably familiar with that story of struggle, but what they *don't* know is that **nobody told me I was ever being evaluated;** my parents **never told** me what the issue was with my learning while growing up.

Because of my situation, my parents had created an environment where excuses were irrelevant; you do something or your do not. There is no "maybe, if I can."

When my parents observed my behavior and considered my personality, both decided against telling me about the problem or telling me that they were intervening with special help—I was better off figuring it out on my own if I had to, but I didn't know "how" to persevere yet; that skill had to be taught.

I remember struggling with certain subjects like math or history, mentioned earlier, and both my mother and father would simplify the issue and tell me to "try harder," or my mom would say "it's mind over matter. You can do anything you set your mind to" as if I had created the "roadblock" intentionally.

At the time, these phrases annoyed me because I was having a really hard time, obviously. However, they were right.

My parents were right not to tell me.

As I got older, my father would say that I "have to get into a mindset of believing that it *is* possible to learn whatever I'm struggling with. If I'm frustrated, take a break. Come back and try to see if I can see it differently. The answer is there. " Their standards were high.

I could've gotten extra help in high school instead of failing two classes' first semester section, but instead they told me nothing was wrong and I should try harder.

So I did.

I tried harder. I was an average student in high school.

Remember in the beginning of this book, how I mentioned Chapman University had rejected me prior to their acceptance of me?

At this time, I had six published books of poetry and I asked Chapman to accept me based on **that merit.**

And they did.

During December 2014, I published two books: *Wisdom 23,* my first memoir that *New York Times* Best-selling

Author Martin Dugard helped me write (whilst I took his class). The second book was *The Drug List,* a poetry collection with over 250 poems in it.

That last semester as an undergrad, I petitioned to take a double course load to graduate; that was seven classes and over forty novels. It was hell, but I did it.

You can do anything you set your mind to...

the mantra of my mother...

The night after applying to Chapaman's graduate school, I received email confirmation informing me that I had been accepted to Chapman University's MFA program—stark contrast to my first application attempt.

Over the summer I found out that I had a remaining GE requirement still outstanding—after I'd already walked...

I asked the dean of my degree's college if I could take an accelerated course concurrently with my first semester of grad school to fulfill the void; Chapman said "Yes, you can do that."

Thus initiating me into my grad school journey and in December 2015, I published four more books: A poetry book, short story collection, second memoir, and my first novel. I published those four books *before* the one-year anniversary of the previous two, which means that I published six books within twelve months of each other. Because I could.

I made a choice at ten years old to keep trying to become the person I wanted to be known as: a genius.

```
Alexa's written expression is also below grade level; thus, she may
benefit from direct instruction in writing mechanics.  Project Read
"Framing Your Thoughts" is an effective program for teaching sentence
structure, punctuation, and paragraph writing.  Such instruction could
be carefully coordinated with Orton-Gillingham instruction after Alexa's
weakness in phonemic awareness has been addressed through the LiPS
program.
```

"...Alexa's weakness in phonemic awareness..."

(from IEP evaluation by the Commonwealth of Massachusetts; 7 years old, 1998)

Now, compare the first results to this one from age twenty-one:

Speech and Language Functioning:
As previously mentioned, Ms. Corbett's expressive vocabulary fell within the High Average range (75th %ile). Her phonemic and semantic fluency fell within the Very Superior range (99th %ile for both).

"Her phonemic and semantic fluency fell within the Very Superior range (99th %tile for both)."
(neuropsychological functioning test; age 21, 2012)

144

I graduated high school, went to college—graduated with my BFA in Creative writing. Then I went to grad school, ~~I am the author of twelve thirteen books.~~ and graduated with my Master of Fine Arts degree in Creative Writing, emphasis on Experimental Fiction—a genre I created with **Boxes.**

Now I understand why my parents let me struggle as a child.

The struggle was good—I needed to learn how to roll with punches before I could throw any of my own.

Dyslexia would've been an excuse—something that told me I wasn't good enough when I could be, and I was, I just had to believe it—really believe in myself. My parents gave me the greatest gift by *not* telling me that I was dyslexic as I struggled, painful as it was to watch, I'm sure. It made me stronger.

They were right not to make it easy; they did me a favor by making it harder than it had to be in the beginning, so that it would be easier for me later. It sounds so backwards and maybe it looks like Stockholm syndrome, but it's not, even though that is exactly what someone with Stockholm syndrome would say. My parents were right when I thought they were wrong, and now that I'm old enough to understand, I know that they gave me limitless potential in exchange for truth. They told me this would happen. They told me I would understand once I was older, and now that I am, I get it.

I grew up wanting so badly to be better than I was, to do better—and I did. My parents created the ability for me to have my own drive to persevere within me whenever my challenges seemed impossible, and riding horses only reinforced that attribute.

If not for Mickey, I'd likely not have learned the necessary discipline required to have ever been successful at anything I've written. His training through riding taught me about real greatness, true humility, determination, and how to believe in myself enough to confront and overcome whatever seemingly-impassable obstacle I might encounter, literally. Some of the fences were actual walls. Riding to a difficult fence requires immense focus and timing, which is a lesson that translates across social paradigms into business and art.

I did not start out as an A-student. I failed at things, often more than once, but I didn't give up did I? No, I kept trying. And I kept trying my way to success until I felt satisfied.

And I think to myself now sometimes to those people who said behind my back that I'd never finish high school, and that teaching me to read was a lost cause…it is such a good thing that I am naturally rebellious; *how do you like me now*?

The moral: Your life is not going to be easy, and nobody ever said it was or would be. And if whatever you are pursuing doesn't present itself with some aspect of difficulty, then you can almost be sure it will not be worth it—good things are easy, but great things are harder to find. So if someone tells you that something you are trying to accomplish is impossible, I challenge you to go show them how it's done and set the example for others to follow.

You can achieve whatever you believe is yours to do—so start doing things and you'd be surprised what you're capable of.

9
Genius Made

Andrew was the most avid reader I ever knew and he will **never get to read anything I've ever written,** because it was his death that catalyzed my entire writing career.

Imagine that.

It's the most tragic story of divine irony. I know that Andrew would be so proud of where I've gone and what I've done since his passing, but it doesn't make me miss him any less.

♠

In terms of the original ploy of this book, what have we learned about genius?

One genius didn't make it past the transition into adulthood, and yet, I was made into who I am *during* my transition into adulthood from his lack thereof.

Andrew's death was either going to make me or break me, and losing him was the worst pain I could ever fathom and I survived it—I am still here; it *made* me genius.
Not "a" genius, but genius; no article "a" leading in.

If everything has its balance, then that means for all the awful things that I've experienced, there's still some pretty wonderful things waiting to happen.

So to answer the question: is a genius born or made?

Made Genius

Maybe it's a little of both for someone who lives in a black and white world.

As for me?

Geniuses don't really exist, remember?

Moments of genius do.
But if they did exist, that's probably a thing I'd make myself to be...

And I finished this book on my 28th birthday, but went back and revised, so it kind of half-counts.

In loving memory of Andrew Corbett

January 27th 1988 – June 15th 2009

www.ingramcontent.com/pod-product-compliance
Lightning Source LLC
Chambersburg PA
CBHW050451290526
45786CB00006B/2241